THE
POSITIVE
BIBLE

THE

POSITIVE

BIBLE

From Genesis to Revelation:

Scripture That Inspires, Nurtures and Heals

Compiled by

KENNETH WINSTON CAINE

 AVON BOOKS  NEW YORK

AVON BOOKS
A division of
The Hearst Corporation
1350 Avenue of the Americas
New York, New York 10019

Copyright © 1998 by Kenneth Winston Caine
Interior design by Kellan Peck
Visit our website at **http://www.AvonBooks.com**
ISBN: 0-380-97471-1

Library of Congress Cataloging in Publication Data:
Bible. English. Selections.
   The positive Bible : from Genesis to Revelation : Scripture that inspires, nurtures, and heals / compiled by Kenneth Winston Caine.—1st ed.
      p.   cm.
   Includes index.
   1. Bible—Quotations. I. Caine, K. Winston.
BS391.2.C342   1998   97-31179
220.5'2—dc21   CIP

First Avon Books Printing: March 1998

AVON TRADEMARK REG. U.S. PAT. OFF. AND IN OTHER COUNTRIES, MARCA REGISTRADA, HECHO EN U.S.A.

Printed in the U.S.A.

FIRST EDITION

QPM   10   9   8   7   6   5   4   3   2   1

COMPILER'S NOTE

Scriptures have been taken from the following sources:

KJV   King James Version
KJVM   King James Version (refers to King James Version Modernized; archaic English has been replaced by equivalent, contemporary phrasing)
NIV   Holy Bible, New International Version
NKJV   New King James Version
RSV   Revised Standard Version
TLB   *The Living Bible*

Some scriptures are marked "compiler's paraphrase." These are not direct quotes from any of the above sources but paraphrases from various sources to give the reader a clear meaning.

Words and phrases that appear in brackets are translations and/or interpretations by the compiler. Some prose phrases have been converted to verse form in order to enhance their clarity and beauty in this abbreviated presentation.

CONTENTS

• NEW TESTAMENT

INTRODUCTION

• USER'S INSTRUCTIONS

Turn to *any* page. You'll find an answer, an instruction, inspiration, encouragement, promise, assurance, or advice—no matter what the question or circumstance!

Or, for quick, specific advice, use the Alphabetical Self-Help Index at the back of the book and instantly locate the verses appropriate for your needs, situations, and challenges at any particular time.

• WHAT WE HAVE HERE

The Bible is rich in stories, histories, genealogies, songs, exaltations, exhortations, laws, and reports.

The Positive Bible is not. *The Positive Bible* is not the Bible. *The Positive Bible* is a piece of the whole. It is an inspirational, abbreviated Bible, specialized for a twenty-first-century environment where we need and demand information distilled into immediately accessible, sound-bite-size pieces.

The Positive Bible offers hope, help, and encouragement. On every page. From Genesis through Revelation. That is its only claim.

• WHY

The Positive Bible came to me in a vision while I was

meditating and praying alone on a beach in Ventura, California, one September night in 1980.

My vision was of an accessible, condensed Bible that strings together—in modern English—every empowering, uplifting, helpful, hopeful, inspiring, and faith-building verse, from Genesis to Revelation, in order. A powerful, thin reference/resource/guide that would easily slip into a briefcase or purse . . . that would cut through the noise of the modern world and instantly offer hope, encouragement, and inspiration to anyone who picks it up.

Here it is.

It took me a long, long time to do it. A lot longer than I thought it would. I ended up in Bible college, and immersed in a fascinating variety of spiritual and religious experiences, along the way. And with the help of some friends who believe this is important work, I even established a part-time ministry devoted to sharing positive, effective spiritual practices.

Obviously for context you'll need to go to the Big Book. And I hope you will. But turn here anytime—and often— for a quick pick-me-up; for an instant dose of timeless wisdom; for spiritual reinforcement.

Read one entry or read them all. Meditate on the words and they will develop great meaning in your life. Every selection is a window, an opening, an opportunity.

May this book inspire you, empower you, and enhance your interaction with the spirit of God—*the soul and creative energy of the universe.*

—Kenneth Winston Caine
December 1996

THE
POSITIVE
BIBLE

OLD
TESTAMENT

GENESIS

And God said, "Let there be light,"
and there was light.
And God saw the light,
that it was good;
and God divided the light from the darkness.

Genesis 1:3–4
KJV

If you do what is right, will you not be
  accepted?
But if you do not do what is right,
sin is crouching at your door;
it desires to have you,
but you must mash it.

Genesis 4:7
NIV

Do not be afraid . . .
I am your shield, your very great reward.

Genesis 15:1
NIV

Is anything too hard for the Lord?

Genesis 18:14
KJV

On the mountain of the Lord it will be provided.

Genesis 22:14
NIV

The LORD,
before whom I walk,
will send His angel with you
and prosper your way . . .

Genesis 24:40
NKJV

And the LORD appeared to him . . . and said,
"Fear not,
for I am with you,
and will bless you . . ."

Genesis 26:24
KJVM

EXODUS

But the more they were oppressed,
the more they multiplied
and the more they spread . . .

Exodus 1:12
RSV

The LORD is my strength and song,
And He has become my salvation;
He is my God, and I will praise Him . . .

Exodus 15:2
NKJV

For I am the Lord that healeth thee.

Exodus 15:26
KJV

. . . he who gathered much had nothing left
   over,
and he who gathered little had no lack.

Every man had gathered according to each
one's need . . .

Exodus 16:18
NKJV

Honor your father and your mother,
that your days may be long in the land
which the LORD your God gives you.

Exodus 20:12
RSV

. . . show me now your way,
that I may know you,
that I may find grace in your sight . . .

Exodus 33:13
KJVM

And the Lord said,
My presence shall go with you,
and I will give you rest.

Exodus 33:14
KJVM

"I will make all my goodness
pass before you,
and will proclaim before you my name 'The
    LORD';
and I will be gracious
to whom I will be gracious,
and will show mercy
on whom I will show mercy.

But," he said, "you cannot see my face;
for man shall not see me and live."

Exodus 33:19–20
RSV

. . . and He has filled him with the Spirit of
   God,
in wisdom and understanding,
in knowledge
and all manner of workmanship
to design artistic works,
to work in gold and silver and bronze,
in cutting jewels for setting,
in carving wood,
and to work in all manner of
artistic workmanship.

Exodus 35:31–33
NKJV

LEVITICUS

. . . today the Lord will appear to you . . .

Leviticus 9:4
KJV

I will send you rain in its season,
and the ground will yield its crops
and the trees of the field their fruits.

Leviticus 26:4
NIV

I will grant peace in the land,
and you will lie down
and no one
will make you afraid . . .

Leviticus 26:6
NIV

DEUTERONOMY

We will stay on the main road. We will not turn
aside to the right or to the left.

Deuteronomy 2:27
NIV

. . . remember the LORD your God:
for it is he that gives you power to get wealth . . .

Deuteronomy 8:18
KJVM

No man should appear before the Lord empty-
handed: Each of you must bring a gift in proportion to
the way the Lord your God has blessed you.

Deuteronomy 16:17
NIV

You shall not pervert justice;
you shall not show partiality;
and you shall not take a bribe,
for a bribe blinds the eyes of the wise
and subverts the cause of the righteous.

Deuteronomy 16:19
RSV

All these blessings will come upon you
and accompany you
if you obey the Lord your God:

You will be blessed in the city
and blessed in the country.

The fruit of your womb will be blessed,
and the crops of your land
and the young of your livestock—
the calves of your herds
and the lambs of your flocks.

Your basket and your kneading dough will be
blessed.

You will be blessed when you come in and
blessed when you go out.

The Lord will grant that the enemies
who rise up against you
will be defeated before you.
They will come at you from one direction
but flee from you in seven.

The Lord will send a blessing on your barns
and on everything you put your hand to.

. . . The Lord will establish you as his holy
people, as he promised you on oath,
if you keep [his] commands . . .
and walk in his ways.

Then all the peoples on earth
will see that you are called
by the name of the Lord,
and they will fear you.

The Lord will grant you abundant prosperity . . .

The Lord will open the heavens,
the storehouse of his bounty,
to send rain on your land in season
and to bless all the work of your hands.

You will lend to many nations
but will borrow from none.
The Lord will make you the head,
not the tail . . .
You will always be at the top,
never at the bottom.

Deuteronomy 28:2–13
NIV

. . . return to the LORD your God,

. . . and obey his voice in all that I command
you this day,

with all your heart and with all your soul;

then the LORD your God will restore your
fortunes,

and have compassion upon you . . .

Deuteronomy 30:2–3
RSV

Choose life,

so that you and your children may live

and that you may love the Lord your God,

listen to his voice,

and hold fast to him.

For the Lord is your life, and he will give you
many years . . .

Deuteronomy 30:19–20
NIV

And the LORD, he it is that does go before you;

he will be with you,

he will not fail you,

nor forsake you:

fear not, and do not be dismayed.

Deuteronomy 31:8
KJVM

Oh praise the greatness of our God. He is the Rock,
his works are perfect, and all his ways are just.

Deuteronomy 32:3–4
NIV

JOSHUA

There shall be no man able to stand against you
all the days of your life:
as I was with Moses, so I will be with you:
I will not fail you, nor forsake you.

Joshua 1:5
KJVM

This book of the law
shall not depart out of your mouth,
but you shall meditate on it day and night,
that you may be careful to do
according to all that is written in it;
for then you shall make your way prosperous,
and then you shall have good success.
Have I not commanded you? Be strong
and of good courage;
be not frightened,
neither be dismayed;

for the LORD your God is with you
wherever you go.

Joshua 1:8–9
RSV

. . . as for me and my house,
we will serve the Lord.

Joshua 24:15
KJV

JUDGES

O Lord! May those who love you
be like the sun when it rises in its strength.

Judges 5:31
NIV

RUTH

May you be richly rewarded by the Lord, the
God of Israel, under whose wings you have come to
take refuge . . .

Ruth 2:12
NIV

The Lord has not stopped showing his kindness
to the living and the dead . . .

Ruth 2:20
NIV

I SAMUEL

He raises up the poor from the dust;
he lifts the needy from the ash heap,
to make them sit with princes
and inherit a seat of honor . . .

I Samuel 2:8
RSV

For the pillars of the earth are the LORD's,
and on them he has set the world.
He will guard the feet of his faithful ones . . .

I Samuel 2:8-9
RSV

As you approach the town, you will meet a pro-
cession of prophets coming down from the
high place with lyres, tambourines, flutes and
harps being played before them, and they will
be prophesying. The spirit of the Lord will come
upon you in power, and you will prophesy
with them; and you will be changed into a different person.

I Samuel 10:5–6
NIV

For the sake of his great name
the Lord will not reject his people,
because the Lord was pleased
to make you his own.

I Samuel 12:22
NIV

But be sure to fear [revere, trust] the Lord
and serve him faithfully with all your heart;
consider what great things he has done for you.

I Samuel 12:24
NIV

In everything he did, he had great success,
because the Lord was with him.

I Samuel 18:14
NIV

May the Lord value my life
and deliver me from trouble.

I Samuel 26:24
NIV

II SAMUEL

And David became greater and greater, for the
LORD, the God of hosts, was with him.

II Samuel 5:10
RSV

And David and all the house of Israel were making merry before the LORD with all their
might, with songs and lyres and harps and tambourines and castanets and cymbals.

II Samuel 6:5
RSV

[The Lord said:]
and I have been with you wherever you went,
and have cut off all your enemies from before
  you;

and I will make for you a great name,
like the name of the great ones of the earth.

II Samuel 7:9
RSV

It may be that the Lord will see my distress
and repay me with good
for the cursing I am receiving today.

II Samuel 16:12
NIV

My God, my rock; in him will I trust:
he is my shield, and the horn of my salvation,
my high tower, and my refuge, my saviour;
He saves me from violence.
I will call on the LORD, who is worthy to be
    praised:
so shall I be saved from my enemies.
When the waves of death compassed me,
the floods of ungodly men made me afraid;
The sorrows of hell compassed me about;
the snares of death prevented me;
In my distress I called upon the LORD,
and cried to my God:
and he did hear my voice out of his temple,
and my cry did enter into his ears.

II Samuel 22:2-7
KJVM

He reached down from on high
and took hold of me;
he drew me out of deep waters.
He rescued me from my powerful enemy,
from my foes,
who were too strong for me.
They confronted me in the day of my disaster;
but the Lord was my support.

II Samuel 22:17–19
NIV

With the merciful You will show Yourself
    merciful;
With a blameless man You will show Yourself
    blameless;
With the pure You will show Yourself pure;
    And with the devious You will show Your-
    self shrewd.

II Samuel 22:26–27
NKJV

For You are my lamp, O LORD; The LORD
shall enlighten my darkness.

For by You I can run against a troop; By my
God I can leap over a wall.

As for God, His way is perfect; The word of the
LORD is proven; He is a shield to all who trust
in Him.

For who is God, except the LORD? And who is a
rock, except our God?

God is my strength and power, And He makes
my way perfect.

He makes my feet like the feet of deer, And sets
me on my high places.

II Samuel 22:29–34
NKJV

You have also given me the shield of Your salvation; Your gentleness has made me great.
You enlarged my path under me; So my feet did
not slip.

II Samuel 22:36–37
NKJV

The LORD lives;
and blessed be my rock;
and exalted be the God
of the rock of my salvation.
It is God that avenges me,
and that brings down the people under me,
And that brings me forth from my enemies:
who has lifted me up on high
above them that rose up against me:
you have delivered me from the violent man.
Therefore I will give thanks to you, O LORD,
among the nations, and I will sing praises to
your name.

II Samuel 22:47–50
KJVM

When one rules justly over men,
ruling in the fear of God,
he dawns on them like the morning light,
like the sun shining forth upon a cloudless
   morning,
like rain that makes grass to sprout from the
   earth.

II Samuel 23:3–4
RSV

I KINGS

Be strong . . .
and keep the charge of the LORD your God,
walking in his ways and keeping his statutes,
his commandments,
his ordinances,
and his testimonies . . .
that you may prosper in all that you do
and wherever you turn . . .

I Kings 2:2–3
RSV

[O Lord] . . .
Give thy servant therefore an understanding
  mind
to govern thy people,
that I may discern between good and evil . . .

I Kings 3:9
RSV

II KINGS

Then the LORD opened the eyes of the young man, and he saw. And behold, the mountain was full of horses and chariots of fire all around . . .

II Kings 6:17
NKJV

[The Lord] . . . promised to maintain a lamp for David and his descendants forever.

II Kings 8:19
NIV

. . . he did that which was right in the sight of the LORD . . .

II Kings 18:3
KJV

Hezekiah trusted in the Lord . . .
He held fast to the Lord
and did not cease to follow him;
he kept the commands
the Lord had given Moses.

And . . . the Lord was with him;
he was successful
in whatever he undertook.

II Kings 18:5–7
NIV

I have heard your prayer,
I have seen your tears;
behold, I will heal you . . .

II Kings 20:5
RSV

And he did what was right in the sight of the
    LORD,
and walked in all the ways of his father David;
he did not turn aside to the right hand or to
    the left.
Not turning aside to the right or to the left.

II Kings 22:2
NKJV

I CHRONICLES

He heeded their prayer, because they put their
trust in Him.

I Chronicles 5:20
NKJV

And David became greater and greater, for the
LORD of hosts was with him.

I Chronicles 11:9
RSV

Success, sucess to you,
and success to those who help you,
for your God is with you . . .

I Chronicles 12:18
NIV

Give thanks to the Lord, call on his name;
make known among the nations what he has
    done.
Sing to him, sing praise to him;
tell of all his wonderful acts.
Glory in his holy name;

let the hearts of those who seek the Lord rejoice.
Look to the Lord and his strength;
seek his face always.
Remember the wonders he has done,
his miracles, and the judgments he pronounced.

I Chronicles 16:8–12
NIV

Sing to the Lord, all the earth!
Tell of his salvation from day to day.
Declare his glory among the nations,
his marvelous works among all the peoples.
For great is the LORD, and greatly to be
   praised . . .

I Chronicles 16:23–25
RSV

Glory and honor are in his presence;
strength and gladness are in his place.

I Chronicles 16:27
KJV

Let the heavens rejoice, let the earth be glad;
let them say among the nations, "The Lord reigns!"
Let the sea resound, and all that is in it;
let the fields be jubilant, and everything in them!
Then the trees of the forest will sing,
they will sing for joy before the Lord . . .

I CHRONICLES

Give thanks to the Lord, for he is good;
his love endures forever.

I Chronicles 16:31–34
NIV

I have been with you wherever you went, and
have cut off all your enemies from before you;
and I will make for you a name, like the name
of the great ones of the earth.

I Chronicles 17:8
RSV

First seek the counsel of the Lord.

I Chronicles 18:4
NIV

Then shall you prosper, if you take heed to fulfil
the statutes and judgments which the LORD
charged Moses with concerning Israel: be strong,
and of good courage; do not dread, nor be
dismayed.

I Chronicles 22:13
KJVM

Be strong and courageous,
and do the work.
Do not be afraid or discouraged,
for the Lord God,
my God,

is with you.

He will not fail you or forsake you . . .

I Chronicles 28:20

NIV

Thine, O LORD, is the greatness,

and the power,

and the glory,

and the victory,

and the majesty:

for all that is in the heaven and in the earth
  is thine;

thine is the kingdom, O LORD,

and thou art exalted as head above all.

I Chronicles 29:11

KJV

Both riches and honor come from You,

and You reign over all;

and in Your hand is power and might;

and it is in Your hand to make great,

and to give strength to all.

Now therefore, our God, we thank you,

and praise Your glorious name.

I Chronicles 29:12–13

KJVM

II CHRONICLES

. . . and the men . . . prevailed,
because they relied upon the LORD . . .

II Chronicles 13:18
RSV

Then Asa cried to the Lord his God and said,
"Lord, there is no one like you
to help the powerless against the mighty.
Help us, O Lord our God, for we rely on you,
and in your name we have come against this
vast [multitude].
O Lord, you are our God;
do not let man prevail against you."

II Chronicles 14:11
NIV

The LORD is with you, while you are with him;
and if ye seek him, he will be found by you;
but if you forsake him, he will forsake you.

II Chronicles 15:2
KJVM

. . . be strong and do not give up;
for your work will be rewarded.

II Chronicles 15:7
NIV

For the eyes of the Lord range throughout the
earth to strengthen those whose hearts are
fully committed to him.

II Chronicles 16:9
NIV

Inquire first for the word of the Lord.

II Chronicles 18:4
RSV

Believe in the LORD your God, and you will be
established; believe his prophets, and you will
prosper.

II Chronicles 20:20
KJVM

So Jotham became mighty, because he prepared
his ways before the LORD his God.

II Chronicles 27:6
KJV

In his distress he sought the favor of the Lord his God and humbled himself greatly before the God of his fathers.

And when he prayed to him, the Lord was moved by his entreaty, and listened to his plea . . .

II Chronicles 33:12–13
NIV

EZRA

And I was strengthened as the hand of the
LORD my God was upon me . . .

Ezra 7:28
KJV

The hand of our God
is upon all those for good who seek Him . . .

Ezra 8:22
NKJV

. . . the hand of our God was upon us,
and he delivered us from the hand of the enemy
and from ambushes by the way . . .

Ezra 8:31
RSV

NEHEMIAH

The God of heaven, he will prosper us;
therefore we his servants will arise and build . . .

Nehemiah 2:20
KJV

Do not grieve,
for the joy of the Lord is your strength.

Nehemiah 8:10
NIV

JOB

Think how you have instructed many,
how you have strengthened feeble hands.

Your words have supported those who have
  stumbled;
you have strengthened faltering knees.

Job 4:3–4
NIV

Yet man is born to trouble, As the sparks fly
upward.

But as for me, I would seek God, And to God
I would commit my cause;

Who does great things, and unsearchable,
marvelous things without number.

He gives rain on the earth, And sends waters
on the fields.

He sets on high those who are lowly, And
those who mourn are lifted to safety.

Job 5:7–11
NKJV

Blessed is the man which God corrects;
so do not despise the discipline of the Almighty.
For he wounds, but he also binds up;
he injures, but his hands also heal.

Job 5:17–18
NIV

But if you will look to God
and plead with the Almighty,
if you are pure and upright,
even now he will rouse himself on your behalf
and restore you to your rightful place.
Your beginnings will seem humble,
so prosperous will your future be.

Job 8:5–7
NIV

God will not cast away a blameless man,
neither will he help the evil doers:

He will fill your mouth with laughing,
and your lips with rejoicing.

Job 8:20–21
KJVM

Yet, if you devote your heart to him
and stretch your hands to him,
if you put away the sin that is in your hand
and allow no evil to dwell in your tent,
then you will lift up your face without shame;
you will stand firm and without fear.
You will surely forget your trouble,
recalling it only as waters gone by.
Life will be brighter than noonday,
and darkness will become like morning.
You will be secure because there is hope;
you will look about you and take your rest in
    safety.
You will lie down, with no one to make you
    afraid,
and many will covet your favor.

Job 11:13–19
NIV

But it is the spirit in a man,
the breath of the Almighty,
that gives him understanding.

It is not only the old who are wise,
not only the aged who understand what is right.

Job 32:8–9
NIV

Behold, God is mighty, and does not despise any;
he is mighty in strength of understanding.
He does not keep the wicked alive,
but gives the afflicted their right.

Job 36:5–6
RSV

He does not withdraw His eyes from the righteous;
But they are on the throne with kings,
For He has seated them forever,
And they are exalted.

Job 36:7
NKJV

But if men are bound in chains,
held fast by cords of affliction,
he tells them what they have done—
that they have sinned arrogantly.
He makes then listen to correction
and commands them to repent of their evil.
If they obey and serve him,
they will spend the rest of their days in prosperity
and their years in contentment.

Job 36:8–11
NIV

PSALMS

Blessed is the man
who walks not in the counsel of the wicked,
nor stands in the way of sinners,
nor sits in the seat of scoffers;
but his delight is in the law of the LORD,
and on his law he meditates day and night.
He is like a tree planted by streams of water,
that yields its fruit in its season,
and its leaf does not wither.
In all that he does, he prospers.

Psalms 1:1–3
RSV

The LORD also will be a refuge for the
oppressed,
a refuge in times of trouble.

Psalms 9:9
KJV

Lord, who may dwell in your sanctuary?
Who may live on your holy hill?

He whose walk is blameless
and who does what is righteous,
who speaks the truth from his heart
and has no slander on his tongue,
who does his neighbor no wrong
and casts no stone on his fellow man,
who despises a vile man
but honors those who fear the Lord,
who keeps his oath even when it hurts,
who lends his money without [excessive
    interest]
and does not accept a bribe against the
    innocent.

He who does these things
will never be shaken.

Psalms 15:1–5
NIV

Lord, you have assigned me my portion
and my cup;
you have made my lot secure.

Psalms 16:5
NIV

Keep me as the apple of your eye,
hide me under the shadow of thy wings,

From the wicked that oppress me,
from my deadly enemies who surround me.

The Lord is my shepherd; I shall not want.

He maketh me to lie down in green pastures;
he leadeth me beside the still waters.

He restoreth my soul;
he leadeth me
in the paths of righteousness
for his name's sake.

Yea, though I walk through the valley
of the shadow of death,
I will fear no evil;
for thou are with me;
thy rod and thy staff they comfort me.

Thou preparest a table before me
in the presence of mine enemies;
thou anointest my head with oil;
my cup runneth over.

Surely goodness and mercy shall follow me
all the days of my life;
and I will dwell in the house of the Lord forever.

The LORD is my light and my salvation;
whom shall I fear?
the LORD is the strength of my life;
of whom shall I be afraid?

Psalms 27:1
KJV

For his anger endures but a moment;
his favor for life;
weeping may endure for a night,
but joy comes in the morning.

Psalms 30:5
KJVM

You are my hiding place;
you will protect me from trouble
and surround me with songs of deliverance.

Psalms 32:7
KJVM

I will instruct you
and teach you in the way you shall go;
I will guide you with my eye.

Psalms 32:8
KJVM

. . . steadfast love surrounds him who trusts in
the Lord.

Psalms 32:10
RSV

My soul makes its boast in the LORD;
let the afflicted hear and be glad.
O magnify the LORD with me,
and let us exalt his name together!

Psalms 34:2–3
RSV

I sought the LORD, and he heard me,
and delivered me from all my fears.
They looked to him, and were lightened:
and their faces were not ashamed.
This poor man cried, and the LORD heard him,
and saved him out of all his troubles.
The angel of the LORD
encamps around those that fear Him,
and delivers them.
O taste and see that the LORD is good:
blessed is the man that trusts in him.

Psalms 34:4–8
KJVM

O fear the LORD, you his saints;
for there is no want to them that fear him.
The young lions do lack,
and suffer hunger;
but they that seek the LORD
shall not want any good thing.

Psalms 34:9–10
KJVM

The righteous cry, and the LORD hears,
and delivers them out of all their troubles.

The LORD is near to the brokenhearted,
and saves the crushed in spirit.

A good person may suffer many problems,
but the Lord will deliver him from them all.

The LORD redeems the soul of his servants:
and none that trust in him shall be desolate.

How precious is Your lovingkindness, O God!
Therefore the children of men
put their trust
under the shadow of Your wings.
They are abundantly satisfied
with the fullness of Your house,
And You give them drink
from the river of Your pleasures.
For with You is the fountain of life;
In Your light we see light.
Oh, continue Your lovingkindness

to those who know You,
And Your righteousness
to the upright in heart.

Psalms 36:7–10
NKJV

Do not fret because of evil men
or be envious of those who do wrong;
for like the grass they will soon wither,
like green plants they will soon die away.
Trust in the Lord and do good;
dwell in the land and enjoy safe pasture.
Delight yourself in the Lord
and he will give you the desires of your heart.

Psalms 37:1–4
NIV

Be still before the Lord and wait patiently for
    him;
do not fret when men succeed in their ways,
when they carry out evil schemes.
Refrain from anger and turn from wrath;
do not fret—it only leads to evil.
For evil men will be cut off,
but those who hope in the Lord
will inherit the land.

Psalms 37:7–9
NIV

The steps of a good man
are ordered by the LORD;
and He delights in his way.

Psalms 37:23
KJVM

Weeping may endure for a night,
but joy comes in the morning.

Psalms 40:5
KJV

Blessed is he that considers the poor;
the LORD will deliver him in time of trouble.

Psalms 41:1
KJVM

O send out Your light and Your truth;
let them lead me . . .

Psalms 43:3
KJVM

God is our refuge and strength,
a very present help in trouble.
Therefore will not we fear,
though the earth be removed,
and though the mountains be carried
into the midst of the sea;
Though the waters thereof roar and be troubled,
though the mountains shake with the swelling . . .

Psalms 46:1–3
KJV

For this God is our God for ever and ever:
he will be our guide even unto death.

Psalms 48:14
KJV

Create in me a clean heart, O God;
and renew a right spirit within me.

Psalms 51:10
KJV

Restore to me the joy of Your salvation,
And uphold me by Your generous Spirit.

Psalms 51:12
NKJV

My soul finds rest in God alone;
my salvation comes from him.
He alone is my rock and my salvation;
he is my fortress, I will never be shaken.

Psalms 62:1–2
NIV

My soul, wait only upon God;
for my expectation is from him.
He only is my rock and my salvation;
he is my defense; I shall not be moved.
In God is my salvation and my glory;
the rock of my strength, and my refuge, is in God.
Trust in him at all times;

people, pour out your heart before him;
God is a refuge for us.

Psalms 62:5–8
KJVM

One thing God has spoken,
two things have I heard;
that you, O God, are strong,
and that you, O Lord, are loving.
Surely you will reward each person
according to what he has done.

Psalms 62:11–12
NIV

Because your lovingkindness is better than life,
my lips shall praise you.
Thus will I bless you.
I will lift up my hands in your name.
My soul shall feast;
and my mouth shall praise you with joy.
On my bed I will remember you,
and meditate on you through the night.
Because you have been my help,
I rejoice in the shadow of your wings.
My soul stays close to you;
your right hand upholds me.

Psalms 63:3–8
KJVM

You care for the land and water it;
you enrich it abundantly.
The streams of God are filled with water
to provide the people with grain,
for you have ordained it.
You drench its furrows
and level its ridges;
you soften it with showers
and bless its crops.
You crown the year with your bounty,
and your carts overflow with abundance.
The grasslands of the desert overflow;
the hills are clothed with gladness.
The meadows are covered with flocks
and the valleys are mantled with grain;
they shout for joy and sing.

Psalms 65:9–13
NIV

But as for me, I will always have hope;
I will praise you more and more.

Psalms 71:14
NIV

But I will hope continually,
And will praise You yet more and more.
My mouth shall tell of Your righteousness
And Your salvation all the day,
For I do not know their limits.
I will go in the strength of the Lord GOD;

I will make mention of Your righteousness,
of Yours only.
O God, You have taught me from my youth;
And to this day I declare Your wondrous works.
Now also when I am old and grayheaded, O God,
do not forsake me,
Until I declare Your strength to this generation,
Your power to everyone who is to come.
Also Your righteousness, O God, is very high,
You who have done great things;
O God, who is like You?
You, who have shown me great and severe
troubles,
Shall revive me again,
And bring me up again from the depths of the
earth.
You shall increase my greatness,
And comfort me on every side.
Also with the lute I will praise you;
And Your faithfulness, O my God!
To You I will sing with the harp, O Holy One
of Israel.
My lips shall greatly rejoice when I sing to You,
And my soul, which You have redeemed.

Psalms 71:14–23
NKJV

Nevertheless I am continually with you;
you have held me by my right hand.

You shall guide me with your counsel,
and afterward receive me to glory.

Psalms 73:23–24
KJVM

Preserve my soul;
for I am holy;
O my God,
save your servant who trusts in you.
Be merciful to me, O Lord;
for I cry to you all day long.
Rejoice the soul of your servant;
for to you, O Lord,
do I lift up my soul.

Psalms 86:2–4
KJVM

Blessed are the people that know the joyful
   sound;
they shall walk, O LORD, in the light of your
   presence.
In your name shall they rejoice all the day:
and in your righteousness shall they be exalted.
For you are the glory of their strength . . .

Psalms 89:15–17
KJVM

So teach us to number our days,
that we may apply our hearts unto wisdom.

Psalms 90:12
KJV

Because you have made the Most High your
    habitation;
No evil shall befall you,
neither shall any plague come near your
    dwelling.
For He shall give his angels charge over you,
to keep you safe in all your ways.
They shall lift you up in their hands,
lest you dash your foot against a stone.
You shall tread upon the lion and cobra;
and you will trample the lion and the serpent.

"Because he has set his love upon me,
I will deliver him," says the Lord.
"I will set him on high,
because he has known my name.
He shall call upon me, and I will answer him;
I will be with him in trouble;
I will deliver him, and honor him.
With long life will I satisfy him,
and show him my salvation."

Psalms 91:9–16
KJVM

Who forgives all my sins;
who heals all my diseases?
Who redeems my life from disaster;
who crowns me with lovingkindness
and tender mercies?

Who provides nourishing food;
so that my youth is renewed like the eagle's?

Psalms 103:3–5
KJVM

The LORD works vindication and justice for all
who are oppressed.

Psalms 103:6
RSV

The LORD is merciful and gracious,
slow to anger and abounding in steadfast love.
He will not always chide,
nor will he keep his anger for ever.
He does not deal with us according to our sins,
nor requite us according to our iniquities.
For as the heavens are high above the earth,
so great is his steadfast love
toward those who fear him;
as far as the east is from the west,
so far does he remove our transgressions from us.

Psalms 103:8–12
RSV

For he satisfies the longing soul,
and fills the hungry soul with goodness.

Psalms 107:9
KJVM

Blessed is the man who fears the Lord,
who finds great delight in his commands.

His children will be mighty in the land;
each generation of the upright will be blessed.
Wealth and riches are in his house,
and his righteousness endures forever.

Psalms 112:1–3
NIV

Even in darkness, light dawns for the upright,
for the gracious and compassionate
and righteous man.

Psalms 112:4
NIV

All goes well for the generous man
who conducts his business fairly.

Psalms 112:5
TLB

God will come to him who is generous
and lends freely,
who conducts his affairs with justice.
Surely he will never be shaken;
a righteous man will be remembered forever.

Psalms 112:5–6
NIV

He does not fear bad news, nor live in dread of
what may happen. For he is settled in his mind
that Jehovah will take care of him. That is why
he is not afraid, but can calmly face his foes. He
gives generously to those in need. His deeds

will never be forgotten. He shall have influence
and honor.

Psalms 112:7–9
TLB

Out of my distress I called on the LORD;
the LORD answered me and set me free.
With the LORD on my side I do not fear.
What can man do to me?
The LORD is on my side to help me;
I shall look in triumph on those who hate me.
It is better to take refuge in the LORD
than to put confidence in man.
It is better to take refuge in the LORD
than to put confidence in princes.
All nations surrounded me;
in the name of the LORD I cut them off!
They surrounded me, surrounded me on
    every side;
in the name of the LORD I cut them off!
They surrounded me like bees,
they blazed like a fire of thorns;
in the name of the LORD I cut them off!
I was pushed hard, so that I was falling,
but the LORD helped me.
The LORD is my strength and my song;
he has become my salvation.
Hark, glad songs of victory in the tents of the
    righteous:

"The right hand of the LORD does valiantly,
the right hand of the LORD is exalted,
the right hand of the LORD does valiantly!"
I shall not die, but I shall live,
and recount the deeds of the LORD.

Psalms 118:5–17
RSV

Open to me the gates of righteousness;
I will go through them,
And I will praise the LORD.
This is the gate of the LORD,
Through which the righteous shall enter.
I will praise You,
For You have answered me,
And have become my salvation.
The stone which the builders rejected
Has become the chief cornerstone.
This was the Lord's doing;
It is marvelous in our eyes.
This is the day the LORD has made;
We will rejoice and be glad in it.
Save now, I pray, O LORD;
O LORD, I pray, send now prosperity.
Blessed is he who comes in the name of the
   LORD!
We have blessed you from the house of the
   LORD.
God is the LORD,

And He has given us light;
Bind the sacrifice with cords to the horns of
the altar.
You are my God, and I will praise You;
You are my God, I will exalt You.
Oh, give thanks to the LORD, for He is good!
For His mercy endures forever.

Psalms 118:19–29
NKJV

Blessed are those whose way is blameless,
who walk in the law of the LORD!
Blessed are those who keep his testimonies,
who seek him with their whole heart
who also do no wrong, but walk in his ways!
Psalms 119:1–3
RSV

Your testimonies also are my delight
and my counsellors.

Psalms 119:24
KJVM

Turn my eyes away from worthless things;
renew my life according to your word.
Psalms 119:37
NIV

Your word is a lamp unto my feet,
and a light unto my path.

Psalms 119:105
KJVM

I lift up my eyes to the hills—
where does my help come from?
My help comes from the Lord,
the maker of heaven and earth.
He will not let your foot slip—
he who watches over you will not slumber . . .

Psalms 121:1–3
NIV

I will lift up my eyes to the hills,
from where will my help come?
My help comes from the LORD,
who made heaven and earth.
He will not let your foot slip;
He who keeps you will not slumber.
Behold, He who keeps Israel
shall neither slumber nor sleep.
The LORD is your keeper;
the LORD is shade upon your right hand.
The sun shall not smite you by day,
nor the moon by night.
The LORD shall protect you from all evil;
He shall protect your soul.
The LORD shall protect your going out
and your coming in
from this time forth,
and even for evermore.
The Lord will keep you from all harm—
He will watch over your life;

the Lord will watch over your coming and going
both now and forever more.

Psalms 121:1–8
KJVM

The Lord has done great things for us;
and we are glad.

Psalms 126:3
RSV

Blessed are all who fear the Lord,
who walk in his ways.
You will eat the fruit of your labor;
blessings and prosperity will be yours.

Psalms 128:1–2
NIV

Where can I go from your Spirit?
Where can I flee from your presence?
If I go up to the heavens, you are there;
if I make my bed in the depths, you are there.
If I rise on the wings of the dawn,
if I settle on the far side of the sea,
even there your hand will guide me,
your right hand will hold me fast.

Psalms 139:7–10
NIV

If I say, "Surely the darkness will hide me
and the light become night around me,"
even the darkness will not be dark to you;

the night will shine like the day,
for darkness is as light to you.

Psalms 139:11–12
NIV

Deliver me, O LORD, from evil men;
preserve me from violent men,
who plan evil things in their heart,
and stir up wars continually.

Psalms 140:1–2
RSV

The LORD is gracious and merciful,
slow to anger
and abounding in steadfast love.
The LORD is good to all,
and his compassion
is over all that he has made.

Psalms 145:8–9
RSV

The Lord is faithful to all his promises
and loving toward all he has made.
The Lord upholds all those who fall
and lifts up all who are bowed down.
The eyes of all look to you,
and you give them their food at the proper time.
You open your hand
and satisfy the desires of every living thing.

The Lord is righteous in all his ways
and loving toward all he has made.

Psalms 145:13–17
NIV

The Lord is near to all who call on him,
to all who call on him in truth.
He fulfills the desires of those who fear him;
he hears their cry and saves them.
The Lord watches over all who love him . . .

Psalms 145:18–20
NIV

PROVERBS

. . . if you cry out for knowledge, and for
   understanding;
If you seek it as silver,
and search for it as for hidden treasures;
Then you will understand the fear of the LORD,
and find the knowledge of God.
For the LORD gives wisdom;
out of his mouth comes knowledge and
   understanding.
He lays up sound wisdom for the righteous;
he is a guardian to them that walk uprightly.
He keeps the paths of judgment,
and preserves the way of his saints.
Then you will understand righteousness,
and judgment, and equity; yes, every good path.
When wisdom enters into your heart,
and knowledge is pleasant to your soul;
Discretion will preserve you,
understanding will keep you;

To deliver you from the way of the evil man,
from the man that speaks evil things . . .

Proverbs 2:3–12
KJVM

Let love and faithfulness never leave you;
bind them around your neck,
write them on the tablets of your heart.
Then you will win favor and a good name
in the sight of God and man.

Proverbs 3:3–4
NIV

Trust in the LORD with all your heart;
and lean not on your own understanding.
In all your ways acknowledge him,
and he will direct your paths.

Proverbs 3:5–6
KJVM

Don't be foolishly proud, respect the Lord, and
avoid evil.
    This will bring health to your body and strength
to your bones.

Proverbs 3:7–8
(Compiler's Paraphrase)

Honor the Lord with your wealth,
with the first fruits of all your crops;

then your barns will be filled to overflowing,
and your vats will be filled with new wine.

Proverbs 3:9–10
NIV

Keep sound wisdom
and discretion
always in sight;
and they will be life to your soul,
and grace to your neck.
Then you will walk safely
whevever you go,
and you will not stumble.
When you lie down,
you will not be afraid;
yes, you will lie down,
and your sleep will be sweet.

Proverbs 3:21–24
KJVM

Have no fear of sudden disaster
or of the ruin that overtakes the wicked,
for the Lord will be your confidence
and will keep your foot from being snared.

Proverbs 3:25–26
NIV

Get wisdom! Get understanding!
Do not forget,
nor turn away from the words of my mouth.
Do not forsake her, and she will preserve you;

Love her, and she will keep you.
Wisdom is the principal thing;
Therefore get wisdom.
And in all your getting, get understanding.
Exalt her, and she will promote you;
She will bring you honor, when you embrace her.
She will place on your head an ornament of grace;
A crown of glory she will deliver to you.

Proverbs 4:5–9
NKJV

When you walk, your steps will not be hindered,
And when you run, you will not stumble.

Proverbs 4:12
NKJV

Do not enter the path of the wicked,
and do not walk in the way of evil men.
Avoid it; do not go on it;
turn away from it and pass on.
For they cannot sleep unless they have done
 wrong;
they are robbed of sleep unless they have made
 some one stumble.
For they eat the bread of wickedness
and drink the wine of violence.
But the path of the righteous is like the light
 of dawn,

which shines brighter and brighter until full
day.

Proverbs 4:14–18
RSV

Put away perversity from your mouth;
keep corrupt talk from your lips.
Let your eyes look straight ahead,
fix your gaze directly before you.
Make level paths for your feet
and take only ways that are firm.
Do not swerve to the right or the left;
keep your foot from evil.

Proverbs 4:24–27
NIV

A slacker's hands produce poverty,
diligent hands produce riches.

Proverbs 10:4
KJVM

. . . the mouth of the righteous
is a fountain of life . . .

Proverbs 10:11
RSV

He who holds his tongue is wise.

Proverbs 10:19
NIV

Your own soul is nourished when you are kind;
it is destroyed when you are cruel.

Proverbs 11:17
TLB

The generous soul will be made rich,
And he who waters will also be watered himself.

Proverbs 11:25
NKJV

He who seeks good finds good will,
but evil comes to him who searches for it.

Proverbs 11:27
NIV

From the fruit of his lips
a man is filled with good things
as surely as the work of his hands rewards him.

Proverbs 12:14
NIV

There is a way of speaking in which your
   words pierce

like thrusts of a sword,
but the wise speak with words that heal.

Proverbs 12:18
KJVM

The Lord is delighted when people speak
truthfully.

Proverbs 12:22
KJVM

Work hard and become a leader;
be lazy and never succeed.

Proverbs 12:24
NIV

Anxiety in a man's heart weighs him down,
but a good word makes him glad.

Proverbs 12:25
RSV

From the fruit of his lips
a man enjoys good things . . .

Proverbs 13:2
NIV

He who guards his lips
guards his soul,
but he who speaks rashly
will come to ruin.

Proverbs 13:3
NIV

The soul of the diligent is richly supplied.
Proverbs 13:4
RSV

Some rich people are poor,
and some poor people have great wealth!
Proverbs 13:7
TLB

The light of the righteous shines brightly . . .
Proverbs 13:9
NIV

Money gained dishonestly will dwindle,
but he who gains money through hard work
can make it grow.
Proverbs 13:11
KJVM

Hope deferred makes the heart sick,
but a long-held desire fulfilled is a tree of life.
Proverbs 13:12
KJVM

The teaching of the wise is a fountain of life,
that one may avoid the snares of death.
Proverbs 13:14
RSV

Every prudent man acts with knowledge,
But a fool lays open his folly.
Proverbs 13:16
NKJV

A wise man thinks ahead;
a fool doesn't, and even brags about it!

Proverbs 13:16
TLB

Poverty and disgrace
come to him
who ignores instruction,
but he who heeds reproof is honored.

Proverbs 13:18
RSV

A scoffer will not find wisdom,
but knowledge comes easy
to a person trying to understand.

Proverbs 14:6
KJVM

The wisdom of the prudent
is to give thought to their ways . . .

Proverbs 14:8
NIV

A simple person believes every word they hear,
but a prudent one gives thought to his steps.

Proverbs 14:15
KJVM

The evil bow down before the good,
the wicked at the gates of the righteous.

Proverbs 14:19
KJV

He who despises his neighbor sins,
but blessed is he who is kind to the needy.

Proverbs 14:20
NIV

He that despises his neighbor sins, but he that
has mercy on the poor is happy.

Don't they who devise evil err? But mercy and
truth shall adorn those that devise good.

Proverbs 14:20–21
KJVM

Those who plan what is good
find love and faithfulness.

Proverbs 14:22
NIV

All hard work brings a profit,
but mere talk leads only to poverty.

Proverbs 14:23
NIV

A patient man has great understanding,
but a quick tempered man displays folly.

Proverbs 14:29
NIV

A relaxed attitude lengthens a man's life;
jealousy rots it away.

Proverbs 14:30
TLB

A peaceful, loving heart gives life to the body,
but envy rots the bones.

Proverbs 14:30
KJVM

He who oppresses a poor man insults his Maker,
but he who is kind to the needy honors him.

Proverbs 14:31
RSV

A soft answer turns away wrath,
But a harsh word stirs up anger.

Proverbs 15:1
NKJV

Your words can bring healing or devastation.

Proverbs 15:4
(Compiler's Paraphrase)

When the eyes sparkle with brightness,
the heart rejoices.
And a good report
makes the bones healthy.

Proverbs 15:30
KJVM

Commit your works unto the LORD,
and your thoughts will be established.

Proverbs 16:3
KJVM

Better is a little with righteousness
than great profits without.

Proverbs 16:8
KJVM

He who gives heed to the word will prosper,
and happy is he who trusts in the LORD.

Proverbs 16:20
RSV

Pleasant words are like a honeycomb,
sweet to the soul,
and health to the bones.

Proverbs 16:24
KJVM

A merry heart doeth good like medicine.

Proverbs 17:22
KJV

He that has knowledge spares his words;
and a man of understanding is of an excellent spirit.

Proverbs 17:27
KJVM

Even a fool who keeps silent is considered wise;
when he closes his lips, he is deemed intelligent.

Proverbs 17:28
RSV

The first to present his case seems right,
until another comes forward and questions him.

Proverbs 18:17
NIV

The tongue has the power of life and death.
Proverbs 18:21
NIV

A man that has friends must show himself
friendly. A friend can be closer than a brother.
Proverbs 18:24
KJVM

To be uninformed is not good;
and to rush carelessly is a sin.
Proverbs 19:2
KJVM

. . . everyone is the friend of him who gives gifts.
Proverbs 19:6
KJVM

. . . he who keeps understanding will prosper.
Proverbs 19:8
RSV

Good sense makes a man slow to anger,
and it is his glory to overlook an offense.
Proverbs 19:11
RSV

He who has contempt for his life is slowly dying.
Proverbs 19:16
(Compiler's Paraphrase)

He who is kind to the poor lends to the LORD,
and he will repay him for his deed.

Proverbs 19:17
RSV

Listen to advice and accept instruction,
that you may gain wisdom for the future.

Proverbs 19:20
RSV

The fear of the LORD leads to life;
and he who has it rests satisfied;
he will not be visited by harm.

Proverbs 19:23
RSV

It is an honor for a man to refuse to perpetu-
ate strife:
but every fool will be meddling.

Proverbs 20:3
KJVM

If you do not plant your fields
while the season is still cold,
you will not produce a crop
by harvest time.

Proverbs 20:4
(Compiler's Paraphrase)

The purposes of a man's heart are like deep waters,
but a man of understanding draws them out.

Proverbs 20:5
NIV

Even a child is known by his deeds,
Whether what he does is pure and right.

Proverbs 20:11
NKJV

Make plans by seeking advice . . .

Proverbs 20:18
NIV

A gossip betrays confidence;
so avoid a man who talks too much.

Proverbs 20:19
NIV

The spirit of man is the lamp of the Lord,
searching all his innermost parts.

Proverbs 20:27
RSV

The plans of the diligent lead surely to
abundance . . .

Proverbs 21:5
RSV

He who closes his ear to the cry of the poor
will himself cry out and not be heard.

Proverbs 21:13
RSV

He who pursues righteousness and love,
finds life, prosperity and honor.

Proverbs 21:21
NIV

He who keeps watch on his mouth and his tongue
keeps himself out of trouble.

Proverbs 21:23
KJVM

A good name
is more desirable than great riches;
to be esteemed
is better than silver or gold.

Proverbs 22:1
NIV

The rich and the poor have this in common,
The LORD is the maker of them all.

Proverbs 22:2
NKJV

Humility
and respect of the Lord
bring riches,
honor
and life.

Proverbs 22:4
KJVM

Whoever is generous will be blessed . . .

Proverbs 22:9
KJVM

Drive out a scoffer and strife will go out,
and quarreling and abuse will cease.

Proverbs 22:10
RSV

He who loves purity of heart,
and whose speech is gracious,
will have the king as his friend.

Proverbs 22:11
RSV

The lazy man says,
"There is a lion outside!
I shall be slain in the streets!"

Proverbs 22:13
NKJV

Pay attention . . . to the sayings of the wise;
. . . it is pleasing when you keep them in
   your heart
and have them ready
on your lips.

Proverbs 22:17–18
NIV

Do not wear yourself out to get rich;
have the wisdom to show restraint.

Proverbs 23:4
NIV

As he thinketh in his heart, so is he.

Proverbs 23:7
KJV

Apply your heart unto instruction,
and your ears to the words of knowledge.

Proverbs 23:12
KJVM

Don't envy evil men but continue to rever-
ence the Lord all the time, for surely you have a
wonderful future ahead of you . . .

Proverbs 23:19
TLB

Do not join those who drink too much wine
or gorge themselves on meat;
for drunkards and gluttons become poor,
and drowsiness clothes them in rags.

Proverbs 23:20–21
NIV

Do not be envious of evil men,
Nor desire to be with them;
For their heart devises violence,
And their lips talk of troublemaking.

Proverbs 24:1–2
NKJV

By wisdom a house is built,
and by understanding it is established;
by knowledge the rooms are filled
with all precious and pleasant riches.

Proverbs 24:3–4
RSV

If you falter in times of trouble,
how small is your strength!

Proverbs 24:10
NIV

PROVERBS

I passed by the field of a sluggard,
by the vineyard of a man without sense;
and lo, it was all overgrown with thorns;
the ground was covered with nettles,
and its stone wall was broken down.
Then I saw and considered it;
I looked and received instruction.
A little sleep, a little slumber,
a little folding of the hands to rest,
and poverty will come upon you like a robber,
and want like an armed man.

Proverbs 24:30–34
RSV

A word fitly spoken
is like apples of gold
in a setting of silver.

Proverbs 25:11
RSV

Let another praise you, and not your own
mouth . . .

Proverbs 27:2
RSV

Correct your son,
and he will give you rest;
yes, he will give delight unto your soul.

Proverbs 29:17
KJVM

Speak up for those
who cannot speak for themselves,
for the rights of all who are destitute.
Speak up and judge fairly;
defend the rights of the poor and needy.

Proverbs 31:8–9
NIV

Behold, I am the Lord, the God of all the living:
is there anything too hard for me?

Proverbs 32.37
KJVM

ECCLESIASTES

For my heart rejoiced in all my labor;
And this was my reward from all my labor.
Ecclesiastes 2:10
NKJV

There is nothing better for a man than that he
should eat and drink, and find enjoyment in his
toil. This also, I saw, is from the hand of God;
for apart from him who can eat or who can have
enjoyment? For to the man who pleases him
God gives wisdom and knowledge and joy . . .
Ecclesiastes 2:24-27
RSV

To every thing there is a season,
and a time to every purpose under the heaven:
A time to be born, and a time to die;
a time to plant,
and a time to pluck up that which is planted;
A time to kill, and a time to heal;
a time to break down, and a time to build up;
A time to weep, and a time to laugh;

a time to mourn, and a time to dance;
A time to cast away stones,
and a time to gather stones together;
a time to embrace,
and a time to refrain from embracing;
A time to get, and a time to lose;
a time to keep, and a time to cast away;
A time to rend, and a time to sew;
a time to keep silence, and a time to speak;
A time to love, and a time to hate;
a time of war, and a time of peace.

Ecclesiastes 3:1–8
KJV

I know that nothing is better for them than to
rejoice, and to do good in their lives.

Ecclesiastes 3:12
NKJV

. . . every man should eat and drink and enjoy
the good of all his labor; it is the gift of God.

Ecclesiastes 3:13
NKJV

When you make a vow to God,
do not delay in fulfilling it.

Ecclesiastes 5:4
NIV

Whoever loves money
never has money enough . . .

Ecclesiastes 5:10
NIV

When God gives any man wealth and possessions,
and enables him to enjoy them, to accept his
lot and be happy in his work—this is a gift of
God.

Ecclesiastes 5:19
NIV

Better is the end of a matter
than its beginning;
and a patient spirit is better than a proud one.

Ecclesiastes 7:8
KJVM

Do not be quick to anger,
for anger resides in the bosom of fools.

Ecclesiastes 7:9
KJVM

A man's wisdom makes his face shine,
and the hardness of his countenance is changed.

Ecclesiastes 8:7
RSV

Whatever your hand finds to do,
do it with all your might . . .

Ecclesiastes 9:10
NIV

The words of a wise man's mouth win him favor,
but the lips of a fool consume him.

Ecclesiastes 10:12
RSV

Cast your bread upon the waters,
for you will find it after many days.

Ecclesiastes 11:1
KJVM

In the morning sow your seed,
And in the evening do not withhold your hand;
For you do not know which will prosper,
Either this or that,
Or whether both alike will be good.

Ecclesiastes 11:6
NKJV

Truly the light is sweet, and a pleasant thing it
is for the eyes to behold the sun.

Ecclesiastes 11:7
KJV

SONG OF SONGS

Do not arouse
or awaken love
until it so desires.

Song of Songs 2:7
NIV

For, lo, the winter is past,
the rain is over and gone.
The flowers appear on the earth,
the time of the singing of birds has come;
and the voice of the turtledove
is heard throughout the land.

Songs of Songs 2:11–12
KJVM

ISAIAH

And it shall come to pass in the last days, that the mountain of the Lord's house shall be established in the top of the mountains, and shall be exalted above the hills; and all nations shall flow unto it.

And many people shall go and say, "Come, and let us go up to the mountain of the LORD, to the house of the God of Jacob; and he will teach us of his ways, and we will walk in his paths." His law shall go forth from Zion, and the word of the LORD from Jerusalem.

And he shall judge among the nations, and resolve disputes for many people: and they shall beat their swords into plowshares, and their spears into pruninghooks: nation shall not lift up sword against nation, neither shall they learn war any more.

O house of Jacob, come, and let us walk in the light of the LORD.

Isaiah 2:2–5
KJVM

If you will not believe,
surely you will not be established.

Isaiah 7:9
KJVM

Behold, God is my salvation;
I will trust, and not be afraid;
for the Lord Jehovah is my strength and my song;
he has become my salvation.

Therefore with joy shall you draw water
out of the wells of salvation.

And in that day you will say,
"Praise the Lord,
call on his name,
tell people of his works
so that all may praise his name.

Sing to the Lord,
for he has done excellent things;
this is known in all the earth."

Cry out and shout,
you inhabitants of Zion,
for great is the Holy One of Israel
who lives in your midst.

Isaiah 12:2–6
KJVM

LORD, you will establish peace for us;
for you have wrought all our works in us.

Isaiah 26:12
KJVM

His God instructs him,
and teaches him the right way.

Isaiah 28:26
NIV

. . . you shall weep no more. He will surely be
gracious to you at the sound of your cry; when he
hears it, he will answer you.

Isaiah 30:19
RSV

And though the Lord gives you the bread of
    adversity,
and the water of affliction,
your teachers will be hidden from you no longer;
but your eyes shall see your teachers.
And your ears shall hear a voice behind you,
    saying,
"This is the way, walk in it,"
when you turn to the right hand,
and when you turn to the left.

Isaiah 30:20–21
KJVM

You will also defile the covering
of your graven images of silver,

And the ornament of your molded images of gold.
You will throw them away as an unclean thing;
You will say to them, "Get away!"

Then He will give the rain for your seed
With which you sow the ground,
And bread of the increase of the earth;
It will be fat and plentiful.
In that day your cattle will feed in large pastures.

Likewise the oxen and the young donkeys
that work the ground
Will eat cured fodder,
Which has been winnowed with the shovel
    and fan.

There will be on every high mountain
And on every high hill
Rivers and streams of waters . . .

Moreover the light of the moon will be as the
    light of the sun,
And the light of the sun will be sevenfold,
As the light of seven days,
In the day that the LORD binds up the bruise
    of His people
And heals the stroke of their wound.

Isaiah 30:22–26
NKJV

He who walks righteously and speaks what is right,
who rejects gain from extortion
and keeps his hand from accepting bribes,
who stops his ears against plots of murder
and shuts his eyes against contemplating evil
—this is the man who will dwell on the heights,
whose refuge will be the mountain fortress.
His bread will be supplied,
and water will not fail him.

Isaiah 33:15–16
NIV

He gives power to the faint;
and to them that have no might he increases
    strength.

Even youths get faint and weary,
and young men utterly fall:

But they that wait upon the LORD
shall renew their strength;
they shall mount up with wings as eagles;
they shall run, and not be weary;
and they shall walk, and not faint.

Isaiah 40:29-31
KJVM

Fear not,
for I am with you.
Be not dismayed;

for I am your God.
I will strengthen you;
Yes, I will help you;
Yes, I will uphold you
with the right hand of my righteousness.

Isaiah 41:10
KJVM

For I the Lord, your God, will hold your
right hand, saying to you, "Do not fear, I will
help you."

Isaish 41:13
KJVM

And I will bring the blind by a way that they
knew not;
I will lead them in paths that they have not
known.
I will make darkness light before them,
and crooked things straight.
These things will I do unto them,
and not forsake them.

Isaiah 42:16
KJV

Fear not, for I have redeemed you;
I have called you by name, you are mine.

When you pass through the waters I will be
with you;

and through the rivers, they shall not over-
  whelm you;
when you walk through fire you shall not be
  burned,
and the flame shall not consume you.

Isaiah 43:1–2
RSV

Forget the former things;
do not dwell on the past.
See, I am doing a new thing . . .

Isaiah 43:18–19
NIV

For I will pour water on the thirsty land, and
streams on the dry ground; I will pour my Spirit
upon your descendants, and my blessing on
your offspring.

Isaiah 44:3
RSV

I have swept away your transgressions like a
  cloud,
and your sins like mist;
return to me, for I have redeemed you.

Isaiah 44:22
RSV

Even to your old age and gray hairs I am he,
I am he who will sustain you.
I have made you and I will carry you;

I will sustain you
and I will rescue you.

Isaiah 46:4
NIV

Those who hope in me
will not be disappointed.

Isaiah 49:23
NIV

The Lord God has given me
his words of wisdom
so that I may know what I should say
to all the weary ones.
Morning by morning he wakens me
and opens my understanding to his will.

Isaiah 50:4
TLB

For the Lord GOD will help me;
therefore shall I not be confounded;
therefore have I set my face like a flint,
and I know that I shall not be ashamed.

Isaiah 50:7
KJV

Therefore the redeemed of the LORD shall
    return,
and come with singing unto Zion;
and everlasting joy shall be upon their head;

they shall obtain gladness and joy;
and sorrow and mourning shall flee away.

Isaiah 51:11
KJV

Shake off your dust;
rise up, sit enthroned . . .
Free yourself from the chains on your neck . . .

Isaiah 52:2
NIV

How beautiful upon the mountains
Are the feet of him who brings good news,
Who proclaims peace,
Who brings glad tidings of good things . . .

Isaiah 52:7
NKJV

"Though the mountains be shaken
and the hills be removed . . .
my unfailing love for you will not be shaken,
nor my covenant of peace be removed,"
says the Lord . . .

Isaiah 54:10
NIV

For as the rain comes down,
and the snow from heaven,
And do not return there,
But water the earth,
And make it bring forth and bud,

That it may give seed to the sower
And bread to the eater,

So shall My word be that goes forth from My mouth;
It shall not return to Me void,
But it shall accomplish what I please,
And it shall prosper in the thing for which I
    sent it.

For you shall go out with joy,
And be led out with peace;
The mountains and the hills
Shall break forth into singing before you,
And all the trees of the field shall clap their
    hands.

Instead of the thorn shall come up the cypress
    tree,
And instead of the brier shall come up the
    myrtle tree . . .

Isaiah 55:10–13
NKJV

I live in a high and holy place,
but also with him who is contrite
and lowly in spirit,
to revive the spirit of the lowly
and to revive the heart of the contrite.

Isaiah 57:15
NIV

Then you will call, and the Lord will answer;
you will cry for help, and he will say:
Here am I.

If you do away with the yoke of oppression,
with the pointing finger and malicious talk,
and if you spend yourselves in behalf of the
    hungry
and satisfy the needs of the oppressed,
then your light will rise in the darkness,
and your night will become like the noonday.

The Lord will guide you always;
he will satisfy your needs in a sun-scorched land
and will strengthen your frame.
You will be like a well-watered garden,
like a spring whose waters never fail.

Isaiah 58:9–11
NIV

And your ancient ruins shall be rebuilt;
you shall raise up the foundations of many
    generations;
you shall be called the repairer of the breach,
the restorer of streets to dwell in.

Isaiah 58:12
RSV

Arise, shine; for your light has come,
and the glory of the LORD has risen upon you.

Isaiah 60:1
KJVM

The Spirit of the Lord God is upon me, because
the Lord had anointed me to bring good news
to the suffering and afflicted. He has sent me to
comfort the broken-hearted, to announce lib-
erty to captives and to open the eyes of the blind.
He has sent me to tell all those who mourn
that the time of God's favor has come, and the
day of his wrath to his enemies. To all who
mourn in Israel he will give:
   Beauty for ashes;
   Joy instead of mourning;
   Praise instead of heaviness.
   For God has planted them like strong and
graceful oaks for his own glory.

Isaiah 61:1–3
TLB

For since the beginning of the world
Men have not heard nor perceived by the ear,
Nor has the eye seen any God besides You,
Who acts for the one who waits for Him.
You meet him who rejoices and does
   righteousness,
Who remembers You in Your ways . . .

Isaiah 64:4–5
NKJV

But now, O LORD, you are our father;
we are the clay, and you our potter;
and we all are the work of your hand.

Isaiah 64:8
KJVM

As a mother comforts her child,
so will I comfort you . . .

Isaiah 66:13
NIV

JEREMIAH

The Lord says:
"If you repent, I will restore you
that you may serve me;
If you utter worthy, not worthless, words,
you will be my spokesman . . ."

Jeremiah 15:19
NIV

"I am with you
to save you and to deliver you,"
says the LORD.
"And I will deliver you out of the hand of the
   wicked,
and I will redeem you out of the hand of the
   terrible."

Jeremiah 15: 20–21
KJVM

I the Lord search the heart
and examine the mind,

to reward a man according to his conduct,
according to what his deeds deserve.

Jeremiah 17:10
NIV

Then I went down to the potter's house and
watched him form a pot on the wheel. But the
pot he was forming was marred, so he transformed it into a different pot, shaping it as
seemed best to him.

Then the word of the LORD came to me, saying, ". . . Cannot I do with you as this potter
does? Like the clay in the potter's hand, so you
are in my hand."

Jeremiah 18:3–6
KJVM

"He defended the cause of the poor and needy,
so all went well with him.
Is that not what it means to know me?"
declares the Lord.

Jeremiah 22:16
NIV

"Am I only a God close at hand,"
says the LORD,
"and not a God far off?

Can anyone hide himself in secret places
so I can't see him?"
says the Lord.
"Do I not fill heaven and earth?"

Jeremiah 23:23–24
KJVM

. . . seek the peace and prosperity of the city to
which I have carried you . . . Pray to the Lord for
it, because if it prospers, you too will prosper.

Jeremiah 29:17
NIV

"I know the plans I have for you," declares the
Lord, "plans to prosper you and not to harm you,
plans to give you hope and a future . . . You
will call to me and come and pray to me, and I
will listen to you . . ."

Jeremiah 29:11–12
NIV

Yes, I have loved you with an everlasting love;
With lovingkindness I have drawn you.
I will build you up again . . .
Again you will take your tambourines
and dance with the joyful.

Jeremiah 31:3–4
KJVM

Therefore they shall come and sing in the
    height of Zion,
Streaming to the goodness of the LORD;
For wheat and new wine and oil,
For the young of the flock and the herd;
Their souls shall be like a well-watered garden,
And they shall sorrow no more at all.

Then shall the virgin rejoice in the dance,
And the young men and the old, together;
For I will turn their mourning to joy,
Will comfort them,
And make them rejoice rather than sorrow.
                                    Jeremiah 31:12–13
                                    NKJV

"I will satiate the soul of the priests with abundance, and my people shall be satisfied with
my goodness," says the LORD.
                                    Jeremiah 31:14
                                    KJVM

Consider this:
I am the Lord,
the God of life and all things living.
Is anything too hard for me?
                                    Jeremiah 32:27
                                    KJVM

Call to me and I will answer you, and will tell you great and hidden things which you have not known.

Jeremiah 33:3
RSV

I will heal them and reveal to them abundance of prosperity and security.

Jeremiah 33:6
RSV

LAMENTATIONS

The steadfast love of the LORD never ceases,
his mercies never come to an end;

they are new every morning;
great is thy faithfulness.

"The LORD is my portion," says my soul,
"therefore I will hope in him."

Lamentations 3:22–24
RSV

The LORD is good to those who wait for him,
to the soul that seeks him.
It is good that one should wait quietly
for the salvation of the LORD.
The Lord is good to those whose hope is in him,
to the one who seeks him;
it is good to wait quietly
for the salvation of the Lord.

Lamentations 3:25–26
RSV

EZEKIAL

A new heart also will I give you,
and a new spirit will I put within you;
and I will take away your heart of stone,
and I will give you an heart of flesh.

Ezekial 36:26
KJVM

And I will put my spirit in you and you will
live . . .

Ezekial 37:14
KJVM

DANIEL

Blessed be the name of God for ever and ever;
for wisdom and might are his.
And he changes the times and the seasons;
he removes kings, and sets up kings;
he gives wisdom to the wise,
and knowledge to them who are understanding.
He reveals the deep and secret things;
he knows what is in the darkness,
and the light dwells with him.

Daniel 2:20–22
KJVM

I thank you, and praise you,
O God of my fathers,
who has given me wisdom and might,
and has made known to me now
what we asked of you . . .

Daniel 2:23
KJVM

How great are his signs!
and how mighty are his wonders! . . .

Daniel 4:3
KJV

. . . the Most High is sovereign over the kingdoms
of men and gives them to anyone he
wishes . . . Your kingdom will be restored to you
when you acknowledge that heaven rules . . .
Renounce your sins by doing what is right, and
your wickedness by being kind to the oppressed. It may be that then your prosperity
will continue.

Daniel 4:25–27
NIV

. . . he is the living God,
steadfast forever,
and his kingdom is that which shall not be
    destroyed,
and his dominion shall be even unto the end.
He delivers and rescues,
and he works signs and wonders
in heaven and in earth . . .

Daniel 6:26–27
KJVM

O Lord, hear! O Lord, forgive! O Lord, listen
    and act!

Daniel 9:19
NKJV

[The angel said:]

... I have come now to give you insight and understanding. As soon as you began to pray, an answer was given, which I have come to tell you, for you are highly esteemed. Therefore, consider the message and understand the vision.

Daniel 9:22-23
NIV

... from the first day
that you set your mind to understand
and humbled yourself before your God,
your words have been heard ...

Daniel 10:12
RSV

HOSEA

Sow for yourself righteousness,
reap the fruit of steadfast love;
break up your unplowed ground;
for it is time to seek the LORD,
till he comes and rains righteousness upon you.

Hosea 10:12
KJVM

But you must return to your God;
maintain love and justice,
and wait for your God always.

Hosea 12:6
NIV

I will heal their faithlessness;
I will love them freely . . .

Hosea 14:4
RSV

JOEL

Return to the LORD, your God,
for he is gracious and merciful,
slow to anger,
and abounding in steadfast love . . .

Joel 2:13
RSV

Fear not, O land;
be glad and rejoice,
for the LORD has done great things!
Fear not, you beasts of the field,
for the pastures of the wilderness are green;
the tree bears its fruit,
the fig tree and vine give their full yield.

Joel 2:21–22
RSV

Be glad, O people of Zion,
rejoice in the Lord your God,
for he has given you
a teacher of righteousness.

He sends you abundant showers,
both autumn and spring rains, as before.

The threshing floors will be filled with grain;
the vats will overflow with new wine and oil.

Joel 2:23–24
NIV

You shall eat in plenty and be satisfied,
and praise the name of the LORD your God,
who has dealt wondrously with you . . .

Joel 2:26
RSV

And it shall come to pass afterward
That I will pour out My Spirit on all flesh;
Your sons and your daughters shall prophesy,
Your old men shall dream dreams,
Your young men shall see visions.
And also on My menservants and on My
    maidservants
I will pour out My Spirit in those days.
And I will show wonders in the heavens and in
    the earth:
Blood and fire and pillars of smoke.
The sun shall be turned into darkness,
And the moon into blood,
Before the coming of the great and awesome
    day of the LORD.
And it shall come to pass

That whoever calls on the name of the LORD
Shall be saved . . .

Joel 2:28–32
NKJV

. . . the LORD will be the hope of his people,
and the strength of the children . . .

Joel 3:16
KJV

AMOS

He that forms the mountains,
and creates the wind,
and reveals his thoughts to man,
that makes the morning darkness,
and treads upon the high places of the earth,
The LORD, The God of hosts, is his name.

Amos 4:13
KJVM

Seek me and live . . .

Amos 5:4
RSV

Seek good, and not evil,
that you may live;
and so the LORD,
the God of hosts,
shall be with you,
as you have spoken.

Hate the evil,
and love the good,
and establish justice
in your community . . .

Amos 5:14–15
KJVM

OBADIAH

. . . as you have done,
it shall be done unto you;
your deeds shall return upon your own head.

Obadiah 1:15
KJVM

JONAH

He said:
"I cried out to the Lord because of my affliction
and he heard me;
out of the belly of hell I cried, Lord,
and you heard my voice."

Jonah 2:2
KJVM

When my life was ebbing away,
I remembered you, Lord,
and my prayer rose to you,
to your holy temple . . .

Jonah 2:7
NIV

MICAH

"Do not my words do good to him who walks
uprightly?"

Micah 2:7
RSV

But truly I am full of power
by the spirit of the LORD,
and of judgment,
and of might . . .

Micah 3:8
KJV

He has showed you, O man, what is good;
and what does the LORD require of you
but to do justice,
and to love kindness,
and to walk humbly with your God?

Micah 6:8
RSV

NAHUM

The LORD is good,
a stronghold in the day of trouble;
and he knows them that trust in him.

Nahum 1:7
KJVM

Now I will break the yoke from your neck
and tear your shackles away.

Nahum 1:13
NIV

HABAKKUK

Though the fig tree may not blossom,
Nor fruit be on the vines;
Though the labor of the olive may fail,
And the fields yield no food;
Though the flock may be cut off from the fold,
And there be no herd in the stalls;
Yet I will rejoice in the LORD,
I will joy in the God of my salvation.
The LORD God is my strength;
He will make my feet like deer's feet,
And He will make me walk on my high hills.

Habakkuk 3:17–19
NKJV

ZEPHANIAH

For the Lord their God will be mindful of them
and restore their fortunes.

Zephaniah 2.7
RSV

The LORD your God in your midst,
The Mighty One, will save;
He will rejoice over you with gladness,
He will quiet you with His love,
He will rejoice over you with singing.

Zephaniah 3:17
NKJV

HAGGAI

. . . be strong, all you people of the land,
says the LORD,
and work.
For I am with you, says the LORD of hosts.
. . . my spirit remains among you;
do not fear.

Haggai 2:4–5
KJVM

From this day on I will bless you.

Haggai 2:19
RSV

ZECHARIAH

Return to me, says the LORD of hosts,
and I will return to you . . .

Zechariah 1:3
RSV

Not by might, nor by power, but by my spirit,
says the LORD of hosts.

Zechariah 4:6
KJVM

Thus says the LORD of hosts, "Render true
  judgments,
show kindness and mercy each to his brother,
do not oppress the widow, the fatherless, the so-
journer, or the poor; and let none of you devise evil
against his brother in your heart."

Zechariah 7:9–10
RSV

For the seed shall be prosperous; the vine shall
give her fruit, and the ground shall give her

increase, and the heavens shall give their dew;
and I will cause the remnant of this people to
possess all these things.

Zechariah 8:12
KJV

I will save you, and you will be a blessing; fear
not, but let your hands be strong.

Zechariah 8:13
KJVM

Ask rain from the LORD in the season of the
   spring rain,
from the LORD who makes the storm clouds,
who gives men showers of rain,
to every one the vegetation in the field.

Zechariah 10:1
RSV

I am the Lord their God
and I will answer them.

Zechariah 10:6
RSV

They will pass through the sea of trouble;
the surging sea will be subdued . . .

Zechariah 10:11
NIV

MALACHI

"I have loved you," says the Lord . . .

Malachi 1:2
RSV

"Bring the whole tithe into the storehouse, that
there may be food in my house. Test me in
this," says the Lord Almighty, "and see if I will
not throw open the floodgates of heaven and
pour out so much blessing that you will not have
room for it."

Malachi 3:10
NIV

. . . for you who revere my name, the sun of
righteousness will rise with healing in its
wings. And you will go out and leap like calves
released from the stall.

Malachi 4:2
NIV

NEW
TESTAMENT

MATTHEW

Blessed are they which mourn:
for they shall be comforted.
Blessed are the meek:
for they shall inherit the earth.
Blessed are they which do hunger
and thirst after righteousness:
for they shall be filled.
Blessed are the merciful:
for they shall obtain mercy.
Blessed are the pure in heart:
for they shall see God.
Blessed are the peacemakers:
for they shall be called the children of God.

Matthew 5:1 9
KJV

You are the light of the world.
A city that is set on an hill cannot be hid.
Neither do men light a candle,
and put it under a bushel,
but on a candlestick;

and it gives light for all that are in the house.
So let your light shine before men,
that they may see your good works,
and glorify your Father in heaven.

Matthew 5:14–16
KJVM

But I say to you, love your enemies,
bless those who curse you,
do good to those who hate you,
and pray for those who spitefully use you
and persecute you,
that you may be sons of your Father in heaven;
for He makes His sun rise on the evil and on
    the good,
and sends rain on the just and on the unjust.
For if you love those who love you,
what reward have you? . . .

Matthew 5:44–46
NKJV

. . . lay up for yourselves treasures in heaven,
where neither moth nor rust consumes
and where thieves do not break in and steal.
For where your treasure is,
there will your heart be also . . .

Matthew 6:20–21
RSV

Therefore I tell you,
do not be anxious about your life,

what you shall eat or what you shall drink,
nor about your body, what you shall put on.
Is not life more than food,
and the body more than clothing?
Look at the birds of the air:
they neither sow nor reap nor gather into barns,
and yet your heavenly Father feeds them.
Are you not of more value than they?
And which of you by being anxious
can add one cubit to his span of life?
And why are you anxious about clothing?
Consider the lilies of the field, how they grow;
they neither toil nor spin;
yet I tell you, even Solomon in all his glory
was not arrayed like one of these.
But if God so clothes the grass of the field,
which today is alive
and tomorrow is thrown into the oven,
will he not much more clothe you, O men of
    little faith?
Therefore do not be anxious, saying,
"What shall we eat?" or "What shall we drink?"
or "What shall we wear?"
For . . . your heavenly Father knows that you
    need [these things].
But seek first his kingdom and his righteousness,
and all these things shall be yours as well.
Therefore do not be anxious about tomorrow,
for tomorrow will be anxious for itself.

Let the day's own trouble be sufficient for the
day.

Matthew 6:25–34
RSV

Ask, and it will be given you;
seek, and you will find;
knock, and it will be opened unto you.
For every one who asks receives;
and he who seeks finds;
and to the one who knocks it will be opened.

Matthew 7:7–8
KJVM

Therefore, whatever you want men to do to
you, do also to them, for this is the Law . . .

Matthew 7:12
NKJV

Those who are well do not need a physician,
but those who are sick.

Matthew 9:12
KJVM

Behold, I send you out as sheep in the midst of
wolves; so be wise as serpents and innocent
as doves.

Matthew 10:16
RSV

Come to Me,
all you who labor and are heavy laden,
and I will give you rest.
. . . for I am gentle and lowly in heart,
and you will find rest for your souls.

Matthew 11:28–29
NKJV

For out of the overflow of the heart
the mouth speaks.
The good man brings good things
out of the good stored up in him . . .

Matthew 12:34–35
NIV

. . . if you have faith as a grain of mustard seed,
you will say to this mountain,
"Move from here to there,"
and it will move;
and nothing will be impossible to you.

Matthew 17:20
RSV

Whatsoever you bind on earth
shall be bound in heaven;
and whatsoever you loose on earth
shall be loosed in heaven.

Matthew 18:18
KJVM

Again I say to you
that if two of you agree on earth

concerning anything that they ask,
it will be done for them
by My Father in heaven.

Matthew 18:19
NKJV

For where two or three are gathered together
in My name, I am there in the midst of them.

Matthew 18:20
NKJV

. . . forgive your brother from your heart.

Matthew 18:35
RSV

. . . with God all things are possible.

Matthew 19:26
KJV

. . . if you have faith and do not doubt . . .
you will say to this mountain
"Be removed
and cast yourself into the sea,"
and it will be done.
And in all things,
if you believe,
you will receive
whatever you ask for in prayer.

Matthew 21:21–22
KJVM

You shall love the Lord your God with all
  your heart,
and with all your soul, and with all your mind.
This is the first and great commandment.
And the second is like it,
You shall love your neighbor as yourself.

Matthew 22:37–39
KJVM

. . . you have been faithful over a few things,
I will make you ruler over many things . . .

Matthew 25:21
KJVM

. . . I am with you always,
even to the end of the world.

Matthew 28:20
KJVM

MATTHEW

MARK

And Jesus said to them, "Follow me and I will make
you become fishers of men."

Mark 1:17
RSV

Like seed sown on good soil, hear the word;
accept it, and produce a crop—
thirty, sixty or even a hundred times what
    was sown.

Mark 4:20
NIV

With the measure you use,
it will be measured to you
—and even more.

Mark 4:24
NIV

Do not be afraid; only believe.

Mark 5:36
NKJV

Whosoever will come after me,
let him deny himself,
and take up his cross,
and follow me.
For whosoever will save his life shall lose it;
but whosoever shall lose his life for my sake
and the gospel's,
the same shall save it.
For what shall it profit a man,
if he shall gain the whole world,
and lose his own soul?
Or what shall a man give in exchange for his
soul?

Mark 8:34–37
KJV

Jesus said to him, "If you can believe, all things are
possible to him that believes."

Mark 9:23
KJVM

If any one would be first,
he must be last of all
and servant of all.

Mark 9:35
RSV

Salt is good; but if the salt has lost its saltness,
how will you season it? Have salt in yourselves, and
have peace one with another.

Mark 9:50
KJVM

. . . all things are possible with God.

Mark 10:27
KJVM

So Jesus answered and said to them,
"Have faith in God.
For assuredly, I say to you,
whoever says to this mountain,
'Be removed and be cast into the sea,'
and does not doubt in his heart,
but believes that those things he says will be done,
he will have whatever he says.
Therefore I say to you,
whatever things you ask when you pray,
believe that you receive them,
and you will have them."

Mark 11:22–24
KJVM

And whenever you stand praying,
if you have anything against anyone,
forgive him,
that your Father in heaven
may also forgive you your trespasses.

Mark 11:25
KJVM

"And you shall love the LORD your God
with all your heart,
with all your soul,
with all your mind,

and with all your strength."
This is the first commandment.
And the second, like it, is this:
"You shall love your neighbor as yourself."
There is no other commandment greater than
these.

Mark 12:30–31
NKJV

Watch and pray so you will not fall into
temptation.
The spirit is willing, but the body is weak.

Mark 14:38
NIV

LUKE

For with God, nothing shall be impossible.

Luke 1:37
KJV

Jesus often withdrew to lonely places and prayed.

Luke 5:16
NIV

Blessed are you who are poor:
for yours is the kingdom of God.
Blessed are you that hunger now:
for you shall be filled.
Blessed are you that weep now:
for you shall laugh.

Luke 6:20–22
KJVM

Love your enemies,
do good to those who hate you,
bless those who curse you,
pray for those who abuse you.

Luke 6:27–28
RSV

And as you wish that men would do to you,
do so to them.

Luke 6:31
RSV

Judge not, and you shall not be judged:
condemn not, and you shall not be condemned:
forgive, and you shall be forgiven.

Luke 6:37
KJVM

. . . give, and it will be given to you;
good measure,
pressed down,
shaken together,
running over,
will be put into your lap.
For the measure you give
will be the measure you get back.

Luke 6:38
RSV

The good man brings good things out of the
good stored up in his heart . . .

Luke 6:45
NIV

Your faith has saved you; go in peace.

Luke 7:50
KJVM

No one lights a lamp and hides it in a jar
or puts it under a bed.
Instead, he puts it on a stand,
so that those who come in
can see the light.

Luke 8:16
NIV

. . . your faith has made you well; go in peace.

Luke 8:48
RSV

And I say to you,
Ask, and it shall be given you;
seek, and you shall find;
knock, and it shall be opened unto you.
For everyone that asks receives;
and they that seek find;
and to those that knock it shall be opened."

Luke 11:9–10
KJVM

Are not five sparrows sold for two pennies?
And not one of them is forgotten before God.
Why, even the hairs of your head are all numbered.
Fear not; you are of more value than many
    sparrows.

Luke 12:6–7
RSV

And Jesus said to his disciples,
"Therefore I say to you,

THE POSITIVE BIBLE

Take no thought for your life,
what you shall eat;
nor for the body,
what you shall put on.
Life is more than food,
and the body is more than clothing.
Consider the ravens:
they neither sow nor reap;
they have neither a storehouse nor barn;
and God feeds them.
And aren't you much more valuable than the
  birds?"

Luke 12:22-24
KJVM

Who of you by worrying
can add a single hour to his life?
Since you cannot do this very little thing,
why do you worry about the rest?

Luke 12:25-26
NIV

Consider how the lilies grow:
they neither toil nor spin;
and yet I say to you,
that Solomon in all his glory
was not arrayed like one of these.
If then God so clothes the grass,
which today is in the field,
and tomorrow is cast into the oven;

how much more will he clothe you,
O you of little faith?

Luke 12:27–28
KJVM

And do not seek what you shall eat
or what you shall drink.
Do not worry about it.
For these are things all people need,
and your Father knows you need them.
Rather, seek his kingdom,
and all these things
will be given to you as well.

Luke 12:29–31
(Compiler's Paraphrase)

Be dressed ready for service and keep your lamps
    burning,
like men waiting for their master to return from
    a wedding banquet,
so that when he comes and knocks
they can immediately open the door for him.

Luke 12:35–36
NIV

From everyone who has been given much,
much will be demanded;
and from the one who has been entrusted
    with much,

much more will be asked.

Luke 12:48
NIV

Blessed is he who comes in the name of the Lord.

Luke 13:35
RSV

For every one who exalts himself will be
  humbled,
and he who humbles himself will be exalted.

Luke 14:11
RSV

Which of you, intending to build a tower, would
not first sit down and figure the cost, and de-
termine whether you can afford to build it? If
you lay the foundation and can't afford to do
any more, all that see it will ridicule you. Saying,
"This man began to build, and was not able
to finish."

Luke 14:28–30
KJVM

Whoever can be trusted with very little can also
be trusted with much . . .

Luke 16:10
NIV

So the Lord said,
"If you have faith as a mustard seed,
you can say to this mulberry tree,

'Be pulled up by the roots and be planted in
  the sea,'
and it would obey you."

Luke 17:6
NKJV

Once, having been asked by the Pharisees when
the kingdom of God would come, Jesus replied, "The Kingdom of God does not come visi-
bly, nor will people say, 'Here it is,' or 'there
it is,' because the kingdom of God is within you."

Luke 17:20–21
NIV

And he told them a parable, to the effect that they
ought always to pray and not lose heart.

Luke 18:1
RSV

And he said, "The things which are impossible with
men are possible with God."

Luke 18:27
KJV

Make up your minds not to worry beforehand
how you will defend yourselves. For I will give
you words and wisdom that none of your adver-
saries will be able to resist or contradict.

Luke 21:14–15
NIV

. . . let the greatest among you
become as the youngest,
and the leader as one who serves.

Luke 22:26
RSV

Pray that you will not fall into temptation.

Luke 22:40
NIV

JOHN

From the fullness of his grace we have all
received one blessing after another.

John 1:16
NIV

But he who does what is true
comes to the light,
that it may be clearly seen
that his deeds have been wrought in God.

John 3:21
RSV

. . . whoever drinks the water I give him
will never thirst.
Indeed the water I give him
will become in him a spring of water
welling up to eternity.

John 4:14
NIV

God is spirit, and those who worship him must
    worship in spirit and truth.

John 4:24
RSV

Jesus said to them, "My food is to do the will of Him who sent Me, and to finish His work. "Do you not say, 'There are still four months and then comes the harvest'? Behold, I say to you, lift up your eyes and look at the fields, for they are already white for harvest!"

John 4:34–35
NKJV

. . . the saying, "one sows and another reaps" is true. I sent you to reap what you have not worked for. Others have done the hard work, and you have reaped the benefit of their labor.

John 4:37–38
NIV

When Jesus saw him and knew that he had been lying there a long time, he said to him, "Do you want to be healed?"

John 5:6
RSV

. . . the Son gives life to whom he will.

John 5:21
RSV

. . . a great crowd of people followed him because they saw the miraculous signs he had performed . . .

John 6:2
NIV

Do not labor for the food which perishes, but for
the food which endures to eternal life . . .

John 6:27
RSV

And Jesus said unto them,
"I am the bread of life:
he that comes to me shall never hunger;
and he that believes on me shall never thirst."

John 6:35
KJVM

It is the Spirit who gives life; the flesh profits
nothing. The words that I speak to you are spirit,
and they are life.

John 6:63
NIV

The words I have spoken to you are spirit and
they are life.

John 6:63
NKJV

Jesus stood up and proclaimed,
"If any one thirst,
let him come to me and drink.
He who believes in me,
as the scripture has said,
'Out of his heart shall flow rivers of living
    water.' "
Now this he said about the Spirit,

which those who believed in him
were to receive . . .

John 7:37–39
RSV

Then Jesus spoke again unto them, saying,
"I am the light of the world:
he that follows me shall not walk in darkness,
but shall have the light of life."

John 8:12
KJVM

. . . my testimony is valid,
because I know where I came from
and where I am going . . .
I stand with the Father who sent me.

John 8:14,16
NIV

Then Jesus said to them,
"When you lift up the Son of Man,
then you will know that I am He,
and that I do nothing of Myself;
but as My Father taught Me,
I speak these things.

"And He who sent Me is with Me.
The Father has not left Me alone,
for I always do those things that please Him."

John 8:28–29
NKJV

And you shall know the truth, and the truth shall
make you free.

John 8:32
KJVM

He who is of God hears the words of God . . .

John 8:47
RSV

. . . if any man be a worshipper of God,
and doeth his will,
him he heareth.

John 9:31
KJV

I am the gate;
whoever enters through me will be kept safe.
He will come in and go out, and find pasture.

John 10:9
NIV

I have come that they may have life, and that
    they may have it more abundantly . . .

John 10:10
NKJV

My sheep hear my voice,
and I know them,
and they follow me:
And I give them eternal life;
and they shall never perish,
nor shall any man pluck them out of my hand.

My Father, who gave them me,
is greater than all;
and no man
is able to pluck them out of my Father's hand.

John 10:27–29
KJVM

. . . believe the miracles . . .

John 10:38
NIV

Jesus said to her, "Did I not say to you that if
you would believe you would see the glory of
God?"

John 11:40
NKJV

I have come as light into the world,
that whoever believes in me
may not remain in darkness.

John 12:46
RSV

Jesus knew that the Father had put all things under
his power, and that he had come from God and
was returning to God.

John 13:3
NIV

Love one another.

John 13:34
KJV

Let not your hearts be troubled;
believe in God, believe also in me.

John 14:1
RSV

. . . the Father who dwells in Me does the works.

John 14:10
NKJV

Most assuredly, I say to you, he who believes in
Me, the works that I do he will do also; and
greater works than these he will do, because I
go to My Father. And whatever you ask in My
name, that I will do, that the Father may be
glorified in the Son.
If you ask anything in My name, I will do it.

John 14:12–14
NKJV

And I will pray to the Father,
and he will give you another Counselor,
to be with you for ever,
even the Spirit of truth,
whom the world cannot receive,
because it neither sees him nor knows him;
you know him,
for he dwells with you,
and will be in you.

John 14:16–17
RSV

. . . you will see me;
because I live, you will live also.
In that day you will know that I am in my Father,
and you in me, and I in you.

John 14:19–20
RSV

Jesus answered, saying,
"If a man love me, he will keep my words:
and my Father will love him,
and we will come to him,
and make our home with him."

John 14:23
KJVM

But the Counselor,
the Holy Spirit,
whom the Father will send in my name,
he will teach you all things . . .

John 14:26
RSV

Peace I leave with you,
my peace I give to you:
not as the world gives, give I to you.
Let not your heart be troubled,
neither let it be afraid.

John 14:27
KJVM

. . . my Father is the gardener.
He cuts off every branch that bears no fruit,

while every branch that does bear fruit
he trims clean
so that it will be even more fruitful.

John 15:1–2
NIV

Abide in me, and I in you.
As the branch cannot bear fruit by itself,
unless it abides in the vine,
neither can you,
unless you abide in me.

John 15:4
RSV

I am the vine; you are the branches.
If a man remains in me and I in him,
he will bear much fruit . . .

John 15:5
NIV

If you abide in me, and my words abide in you,
ask whatever you will, and it shall be done for you.
By this my Father is glorified, that you bear
    much fruit,
and so prove to be my disciples.
As the Father has loved me, so have I loved you;
abide in my love.

John 15:7–9
RSV

This is my commandment, that you love one another as I have loved you. Greater love has no
man than this, that a man lay down his life for
his friends. You are my friends if you do what
I command you.

John 15:12–14
RSV

If you belonged to the world,
it would love you as its own.
As it is, you do not belong to the world
but I have chosen you out of the world . . .

John 15:19
NIV

I have yet many things to say to you,
but you cannot bear them now.
When the Spirit of truth comes,
he will guide you into all the truth;
for he will not speak on his own authority,
but whatever he hears he will speak,
and he will declare to you the things that are
    to come.

John 16:12–13
RSV

And in that day you will ask Me nothing. Most
assuredly, I say to you, whatever you ask the
Father in My name He will give you.

Until now you have asked nothing in My name.
Ask, and you will receive, that your joy may be
full . . .

In that day you will ask in My name,
and I do not say to you that I shall pray the
Father for you; for the Father Himself loves
you . . .

John 16:23–24, 26–27
NKJV

. . . in me you may have peace. In the world you
have tribulation; but be of good cheer, I have
overcome the world.

John 16:33
RSV

[Jesus said] ". . . this is eternal life, that they
may know You, the only true God . . ."

John 17:3
NKJV

Make them holy by the truth;
your word is truth.
As you sent me into the world,
I have sent them into the world.

John 17:17–18
NIV

I do not pray for these alone, but also for those
who will believe in Me through their word;

that they all may be one, as You, Father, are in Me, and I in You; that they also may be one in Us . . .

John 17:20–21
NKJV

ACTS

"In the last days," God says,
"I will pour out my Spirit on all people.
Your sons and daughters will prophesy,
your young men will see visions,
your old men will dream dreams.

"Even on my servants, both men and women,
I will pour out my Spirit in those days,
and they will prophesy.

"I will show wonder in the heaven above
and signs on the earth below,
blood and fire and clouds of smoke.

"The sun will be turned to darkness
and the moon to blood
before the coming of the great and glorious day
of the Lord.

"And everyone who calls
on the name of the Lord will be saved."

Acts 2:17–21
NIV

I saw the Lord always before me.
Because he is at my right hand,
I will not be shaken.
Therefore my heart is glad and my tongue rejoices;
my body also will live in hope.

Acts 2:25–26
NIV

You have made known to me the ways of life;
you shall make me full of joy with your presence.

Acts 2:28
KJVM

It is by the name of Jesus Christ of Nazareth . . .
that this man stands before you completely healed.

Acts 4:10
NIV

Stretch out your hand to heal and perform miraculous signs and wonders through the name of
your holy servant Jesus.

Acts 4:30
NIV

And when they had prayed, the place where they
were assembled together was shaken; and they
were all filled with the Holy Spirit, and they

spoke the word of God with boldness. Now the multitude of those who believed were of one heart and one soul . . .

Acts 4:31–32
NKJV

We must obey God rather than men.

Acts 5:29
RSV

God was with him,
And delivered him out of all his afflictions,
and gave him favor and wisdom . . .

Acts 7:9–10
KJV

And the angel replied, "Your prayers and charities have not gone unnoticed by God."

Acts 10:4
TLB

And Peter opened his mouth and said: "Truly I perceive that God shows no partiality, but in every nation any one who fears him and does what is right is acceptable to him."

Acts 10:34–35
RSV

. . . an angel of the Lord appeared, and a light shone . . .

Acts 12:7
RSV

. . . if you have a message of encouragement
for the people, please speak.

Acts 13:15
NIV

Therefore, brethren, know that through Jesus the
forgiveness of sins is preached.

Acts 13:38
KJVM

He has shown kindness
by giving you rain from heaven
and crops in their seasons;
he provides you with plenty of food
and fills your hearts with joy.

Acts 14:17
NIV

The God who made the world
and everything in it
is the Lord of heaven and earth
and does not live in temples built by hands . . .
he gives all men life and breath and everything else.

Acts 17:24–35
NIV

For in him we live,
and move,
and have our being;

as certain . . . of your own poets have said,
"For we are also his offspring."

Acts 17:28
KJV

Now the Lord spoke to Paul in the night by
 a vision,
"Do not be afraid,
but speak, and do not keep silent;
for I am with you,
and no one will attack you to hurt you;
for I have many people in this city."

Acts 18:9
KJVM

ROMANS

The just shall live by faith.

Romans 1:17
KJV

God will give to each person according to what
he has done. To those, who by persistence in
doing good, seek glory, honor and immortality, he
will give eternal life . . . [There will be] . . .
glory, honor and peace for everyone who does
good.

Romans 2:6–7, 10
NIV

[Jesus] died for our sins
and rose again
to make us right with God,
filling us with God's goodness.

Romans 4:25
TLB

. . . we have peace with God through our Lord
Jesus Christ.

Romans 5:1
KJV

Therefore, since we are justified by faith, we have
peace with God through our Lord Jesus Christ.
Through him we have obtained access to this
grace in which we stand, and we rejoice in our
hope of sharing the glory of God.
More than that, we rejoice in our sufferings,
knowing that suffering produces endurance,
and endurance produces character, and character
produces hope, and hope does not disappoint
us, because God's love has been poured into our
hearts through the Holy Spirit which has been
given to us.

Roman 5:1–5
RSV

. . . much more will those who receive the abundance of grace and the free gift of righteousness reign in life through the one man Jesus
Christ.

Romans 5:17
RSV

We were . . . buried with him [Christ] through
baptism into death in order that just as Christ

was raised from the dead through the glory of the
Father, we too may live a new life.

Romans 6:4
NIV

. . . our old self was crucified with him so that
the body of sin might be rendered powerless,
that we should no longer be slaves to sin . . .

Romans 6:6
NIV

. . . give yourselves completely to God
—every part of you—
for . . . you want to be tools in the hands of God
to be used for his good purposes.

Romans 6:13
NIV

There is therefore now no condemnation
to them who are in Christ Jesus,
who walk not after the flesh,
but after the Spirit.

Romans 8:1
KJV

. . . those who live according to the Spirit
set their minds on the things of the Spirit.
. . . to set the mind on the Spirit is life and peace.

Romans 8:5–6
RSV

ROMANS

If Christ is in you . . . your spirit is alive
because of righteousness.

Romans 8:10
NIV

For all who are led by the Spirit of God are sons
of God. For you did not receive the spirit of
slavery to fall back into fear, but you have received the spirit of sonship . . .

Romans 8:14–15
RSV

And we know that all things work together for
good to them that love God, to them who are
the called according to his purpose.

Romans 8:28
KJV

. . . If God is for us, who can be against us?

Romans 8:31
NKJV

Who shall separate us from the love of Christ?
Shall tribulation, or distress,
or persecution, or famine,
or nakedness, or peril, or sword?
. . . Nay, in all these things
we are more than conquerors
through him that loved us.

Romans 8:35, 37
KJV

For I am persuaded, that neither death, nor life,
nor angels, nor principalities,
nor powers,
nor things present, nor things to come,
Nor height, nor depth,
nor any other creature,
shall be able to separate us from the love of God,
which is in Christ Jesus our Lord.

Romans 8:38–39
KJV

And whoever believes on Him will not be put to
shame.

Romans 9:33
NKJV

. . . the same Lord is Lord of all and bestows his
riches upon all who call upon him.

Romans 10:12
RSV

. . . if the root is holy, so are the branches.

Romans 11:16
NKJV

. . . from him
and through him
and to him
are all things . . .

Romans 11:36
RSV

Offer your bodies as living sacrifice, holy and
pleasing, to God . . .

Romans 12:1
NIV

And do not be conformed to this world
but be transformed by the renewing of your mind,
that you may prove what is that good
and acceptable and perfect will of God.

Romans 12:2
NKJV

We each have different gifts,
according to the grace given us.
If a man's gift is prophesying,
let him use it in proportion to his faith.
If it is serving, let him serve;
if it is teaching, let him teach;
if it is encouraging, let him encourage;
if it is contributing to the needs of others,
let him give generously;
if it is leadership, let him govern diligently;
if it is showing mercy, let him do it cheerfully.

Romans 12:6–8
NIV

Love must be sincere.
Hate what is evil; cling to what is good.
Be devoted to one another in brotherly love.
Honor one another above yourselves.
Never be lacking in zeal,

but keep your spiritual fervor,
serving the Lord.

Romans 12:9–11
NIV

Be joyful in hope,
patient in affliction,
faithful in prayer.

Romans 12:12
NIV

Bless those who persecute you;
bless and do not curse.

Romans 12:14
NKJV

Rejoice with those who rejoice;
work with those who work.
Live in harmony with one another.
Do not be proud,
but be willing to associate
with people of low position
Do not be conceited.

Romans 12:15–16
NIV

Repay no one evil for evil.
Have regard for good things in the sight of all men.

Romans 12:17
NKJV

If it is possible, as much as depends on you,
live peaceably with all men.

Romans 12:18
NKJV

Beloved, never avenge yourselves, but leave it to
the wrath of God; for it is written, "Vengeance
is mine, I will repay, says the Lord."
  No, "if your enemy is hungry, feed him; if he
is thirsty, give him drink; for by so doing you
will heap burning coals upon his head."

Romans 12:19–20
RSV

Do not be overcome by evil,
but overcome evil with good.

Romans 12:21
NKJV

Give everyone what you owe them:
If you owe taxes, pay taxes;
if revenue, then revenue,
if respect, then respect,
if honor, then honor.

Romans 13:7
NIV

". . . love your neighbor as yourself."
Love does no harm to a neighbor . . .

Romans 13:9–10
NKJV

The night is nearly over, the day is almost here.
So let us put aside the deeds of darkness
and put on the armor of light.

Romans 13:12
NIV

. . . whether we live or die, we are the Lord's.
. . . Therefore let us not judge one another
anymore, but rather resolve this, not to put
a stumbling block or a cause to fall in our
brother's way.

Romans 14:8, 13
NKJV

For the kingdom of God is . . . righteousness and
peace and joy in the Holy Spirit; he who thus
serves Christ is acceptable to God and approved
by men. Let us then pursue what makes for
peace and for mutual upbuilding.

Romans 14:17–19
RSV

We who are strong
ought to bear with the failings of the weak
and not to please ourselves.
Each of us
should please his neighbor for his good,
to build him up.

Romans 15:1–2
NIV

For whatever things were written before were written for our learning, that we through the patience and comfort of the Scriptures might have hope.

Romans 15:4
NKJV

Now I urge you, brethren, note those who cause divisions and offenses . . . and avoid them.

Romans 16:17
NKJV

. . . be wise about what is good, and innocent about what is evil.

Romans 16:19
NIV

I CORINTHIANS

Grace to you and peace from God our Father and
the Lord Jesus Christ.

I give thanks to God always for you because of
the grace of God which was given you in Christ
Jesus, that in every way you were enriched in him
with all speech and all knowledge . . .
[He] will sustain you to the end . . .

I Corinthians 1:3–5, 8
RSV

. . . the foolishness of God is wiser than men;
and the weakness of God is stronger than men.

I Corinthians 1:25
KJV

"Let him who boasts, boast of the Lord."

I Corinthians 1:31
RSV

Do you not know that
you are the temple of God

and that the Spirit of God
dwells in you?

I Corinthians 3:16
NKJV

"All things are lawful for me," but not all things
are helpful. "All things are lawful for me," but
I will not be enslaved by anything.

I Corinthians 6:12
RSV

. . . every man has his proper gift of God:
One has this gift, another has that.

I Corinthians 7:7
KJVM

. . . if one loves God, one is known by him.

I Corinthians 8:3
RSV

Don't you know that in a race,
everyone runs,
but only one runner gets the prize.
When you run, run for the prize.

I Corinthians 9:24
KJVM

God . . . will not let you be tempted beyond what
you can bear. But when you are tempted, he
will also provide a way so that you can stand
up under it.

I Corinthians 10:13
NIV

THE POSITIVE BIBLE

"All things are lawful,"
but not all things are helpful.
"All things are lawful,"
but not all things build up.
Let no one seek his own good,
but the good of his neighbor.

I Corinthians 10:23–24
RSV

. . . whatever you do, do it for the glory of God.

I Corinthians 10:31
NIV

There are diversities of gifts,
but the same Spirit.
There are differences of ministries,
but the same Lord.
And there are diversities of activities,
but it is the same God who works all in all.
   . . . the manifestation of the Spirit is given to
      each one
for the profit of all:
for to one is given the word of wisdom
through the Spirit,
to another the word of knowledge
through the same Spirit,
to another faith by the same Spirit,
to another gifts of healing by the same Spirit,
to another the working of miracles,
to another prophecy,

to another discerning of spirits,
to another different kinds of tongues,
to another the interpretation of tongues.
But one and the same Spirit works all these things,
distributing to each one individually as He wills.
For as the body is one and has many members,
but all the members of that one body, being many,
are one body,
so also is Christ.

I Corinthians 12:4–12
NKJV

As it is, there are many parts, yet one body.
. . . If one member suffers, all suffer together;
if one member is honored, all rejoice together.

I Corinthians 12:20, 26
RSV

Though I speak with the tongues of men and
    of angels,
and have not love,
I become only a resounding gong,
or a tinkling cymbal.
And though I have the gift of prophecy,
and understand all mysteries,
and all knowledge;
and though I have all faith,
so that I could remove mountains,
and have not love,
I am nothing.

And though I bestow all my goods to feed the poor,
and though I give my body to be burned,
and have not love,
I gain nothing.

I Corinthians 13:1–3
KJVM

Love is patient, love is kind.
It does not envy, it does not boast, it is not proud.
It is not rude, it is not self-seeking, it is not easily
    angered,
it keeps no record of wrongs.
Love does not delight in evil but rejoices with
    the truth.
It always protects, always trusts,
always hopes, always perseveres.
Love never fails . . .

I Corinthians 13:4–8
NIV

Keep faith, hope and love alive in you, these three;
but the greatest of these is love.

I Corinthians 13:13
KJVM

Make love your aim,
and earnestly desire the spiritual gifts,
especially that you may prophesy.

I Corinthians 14:1
RSV

. . . everyone who prophesies speaks to men for
their strengthening, encouragement and comfort.

I Corinthians 14:3
NIV

What am I to do?
I will pray with the spirit
and I will pray with the mind also;
I will sing with the spirit
and I will sing with the mind also.

I Corinthians 14:15
RSV

What is it then?
I will pray with the spirit,
and I will pray with the understanding also:
I will sing with the spirit,
and I will sing with the understanding also.

I Corinthians 14:15
KJV

. . . hold firmly to the word . . .

I Corinthians 15:2
NIV

Do not be misled: Bad company corrupts good
character.

I Corinthians 15:33
NIV

Therefore, my beloved brothers,
be steadfast,
unmoveable,

always abounding in the work of the Lord,
for your labor is not in vain in the Lord.

I Corinthians 15:58
KJVM

. . . for a wide door for effective work has
opened to me . . .

I Corinthians 16:9
RSV

Be on your guard;
stand firm in the faith;
be men of courage;
be strong.
Do everything in love.

I Corinthians 16:13
NIV

II CORINTHIANS

Blessed be God,
the Father of our Lord Jesus Christ,
the Father of mercy,
and the God of all comfort;
who comforts us in all our troubles,
so that we may comfort those
who are in any trouble,
with the comfort we ourselves
have received from God.

II Corinthians 1:3–4
KJVM

But this happened
that we might not rely on ourselves
but on God . . .
on him we have set our hope . . .

II Corinthians 1:9–10
NIV

. . . show that you are a letter from Christ . . .
written not with ink
but with the Spirit of the Living God,

THE POSITIVE BIBLE

not on tablets of stone
but on tablets of human hearts.

II Corinthians 3:3
NIV

Not that we are competent of ourselves
to claim anything as coming from us;
our competence is from God . . .

II Corinthians 3:5
RSV

We are troubled on every side, yet not distressed;
we are perplexed, but not in despair;
persecuted, but not forsaken;
cast down, but not destroyed;
Always bearing in us the death of Jesus,
so that the life of Jesus
also might manifest in us.

II Corinthians 4:8–10
KJVM

Do not lose heart.
Though outwardly we are wasting away,
yet inwardly we are being renewed day by day.

II Corinthians 4:16
NIV

For our light affliction,
which is but for a moment,
is working for us a far more exceeding and
 eternal weight of glory,

while we do not look at the things which are seen,
but at the things which are not seen . . .

II Corinthians 4:17–18
NKJV

For we walk by faith,
not by sight.

II Corinthians 5:7
KJV

Therefore
if any man is in Christ,
he is a new creature:
old things pass away;
behold, all things become new.

II Corinthians 5:17
KJVM

. . . as servants of God
we commend ourselves in every way:
in great endurance;
in troubles, hardships and distresses;
in beatings, imprisonments and riots;
in hard work, sleepless nights and hunger,
in purity, understanding, patience and kindness,
in the Holy Spirit and in sincere love,
in truthful speech and in the power of God;
with weapons of righteousness in the right hand
    and in the left.

Through glory and dishonor,
bad report and good report;
genuine, yet regarded as impostors,
known, yet regarded as unknown;
dying, and yet we live on,
beaten, and yet not killed;
sorrowful, yet always rejoicing;
poor yet making many rich;
having nothing and yet possessing everything.

II Corinthians 6:4–10
NIV

. . . for you are the temple of the living God;
as God has said,
"I will dwell in them,
and walk in them;
and I will be their God,
and they shall be my people."

II Corinthians 6:16
KJVM

. . . let us purify ourselves from everything that
contaminates body and spirit . . .

II Corinthians 7:1
NIV

I rejoice, because I have perfect confidence in you.

II Corinthians 7:16
RSV

Whoever sows sparingly will also reap sparingly,
and whoever sows generously will also reap
generously.
Each man should give
what he has decided in his heart to give
not reluctantly or under compulsion,
for God loves a cheerful giver.
And God is able to make all grace abound to you,
so that in all things
at all times,
having all that you need,
you will abound in every good work.
. . . Now he who supplies seed to the sower
and bread for food
will also supply and increase your store of seed
and will enlarge the harvest of your
righteousness.
You will be made rich in every way
so that you can be generous on every occasion . . .

II Corinthians 9:6–8, 10–11
NIV

For though we live in the world,
we do not wage war as the world does.
The weapons we fight with
are not the weapons of the world.
On the contrary
they have divine power to demolish strongholds.
We demolish arguments and every pretension

that sets itself up against the knowledge of God,
and we take captive every thought
to make it obedient to Christ.

II Corinthians 10:3–5
NIV

. . . there was given me a thorn in my flesh . . .
to torment me. Three times I pleaded with the
Lord to take it away from me. But he said to me,
"My grace is sufficient for you, for my power
is made perfect in [overcoming] weakness" . . .

II Corinthians 12:7–8
NIV

. . . we have been speaking in the sight of God as
those in Christ; and everything we do, dear
friends, is for your strengthening.

II Corinthians 12:19
NIV

Finally, people,
aim for perfection . . .
be of good comfort,
be of one mind,
live in peace;
and the God of love and peace
shall be with you.

II Corinthians 13:11
KJVM

[May] The grace of the Lord Jesus Christ
and the love of God
and the fellowship of the Holy Spirit
be with you . . .

II Corinthians 13:14
RSV

GALATIANS

Grace and peace to you from God the Father,
and from our Lord Jesus Christ,
who gave himself for our sins,
that he might rescue us from this present evil age,
according to the will of God and our Father:
To whom be glory for ever and ever. Amen.

Galatians 1:3
KJVM

Am I now trying to win the approval of men,
or of God?
Or am I trying to please men?
If I were still trying to please men,
I would not be a servant of Christ.

Galatians 1:10
NIV

. . . by faith we eagerly await
through the Spirit
the righteousness
for which we hope.

. . . The only thing that counts
is faith expressing itself through love.

Galatians 5:5–6
NIV

You have been granted total freedom;
but do not use your freedom hedonistically;
rather to lovingly serve one another.
For all the law is fulfilled in one statement:
"Love your neighbor as yourself."

Galatians 5:13
KJVM

But the fruit of the Spirit
is love, joy, peace,
patience, gentleness, goodness,
faith, kindness, self-control . . .
If we live in the Spirit,
let us also walk in the Spirit.
Let us not be conceited,
provoking one another,
envying one another.

Galatians 5: 22–23, 25–26
KJVM

And let us not weary of doing good:
for in due season we shall reap,
if we do not lose heart.
As we have opportunity therefore,

let us do good to all people,
especially to them
who are of the household of faith.

Galatians 6:9–10
KJVM

EPHESIANS

May the God of our Lord Jesus Christ,
the Father of glory,
give you the spirit of wisdom and revelation
in your knowledge of him:
so you see with enlightened understanding
and know the hope to which he calls you,
as evidenced in the saints
who inherited his riches and glory,
and may you know
his extraordinary, unsurpassable power
ever flowing to us who believe,
the same power that raised Christ from the
    grave . . .

Ephesians 1:17–20
(Compiler's Paraphrase)

. . . because of his great love for us,
God, who is rich in love,
made us alive with Christ . . .

Ephesians 2:4–5
NIV

For we are His workmanship,
created in Christ Jesus for good works,
which God prepared beforehand
that we should walk in them.

Ephesians 2:10
NKJV

For He Himself is our peace . . .

Ephesians 2:14
NKJV

And in him you are being built
as a dwelling in which God lives
in spirit.

Ephesians 2:22
KJVM

I pray that he would grant you,
from his glorious riches,
strength with power
through his Spirit within you;
that Christ may dwell in your hearts by faith;
that you, being rooted and grounded in love,
may be able to comprehend,
as have all the saints,
how wide and long and deep and high
is the love of Christ,
and know this love
which surpasses knowledge,
so you might be filled
with all the fullness of God.

Now unto him who is able to do
exceeding abundantly above all that we ask or
  think,
by his power that works in us,
to him be glory in the church
and in Christ Jesus
throughout all ages,
world without end. Amen.

Ephesians 3:16–21
KJVM

. . . live life worthy of your calling from God;
With all humility and gentleness,
with patience,
bearing one another in love;
endeavoring to keep the unity of the Spirit
in the bond of peace.
There is one body,
and one Spirit . . .
One Lord, one faith, one baptism,
One God and Father of all,
who is above all,
and through all,
and in you all.

Ephesians 4:1–6
KJVM

And he gave some the calling to be apostles;
and some, prophets;

and some, evangelists;
and some, pastors and teachers;
for preparing his people
for the work of the ministry,
for building up the body of Christ:
till we all attain a unity of the faith,
and of the knowledge of the Son of God,
and achieve perfection,
as measured by the stature
of the fullness of Christ.

Ephesians 4:11–13
KJVM

You were taught,
with regard to your former way of life,
to put off your old self,
which is being corrupted by its deceitful desires;
to be made new in the attitude of your minds;
and to put on the new self,
created to be like God
in true righteousness and holiness.

Ephesians 4:22–24
NIV

Do not let any unwholesome talk
come out of your mouth,
but only what is helpful for building others up
according to their needs,
that it may benefit those who listen.

Ephesians 4:29
NIV

EPHESIANS

Let go of all bitterness,
and wrath,
and anger,
and brooding together,
and evil speaking,
and all malice;
and be kind one to another,
tenderhearted,
forgiving one another,
even as God for Christ's sake
has forgiven you.

Ephesians 4:31–32
KJVM

Therefore be imitators of God,
as beloved children.
And walk in love,
as Christ loved us . . .

Ephesians 5:1–2
RSV

. . . now you are light in the Lord.
Walk as children of light
(for the fruit of the Spirit is in all goodness,
righteousness, and truth),
finding out what is acceptable to the Lord.
And have no fellowship
with the unfruitful works of darkness,
but rather expose them.

Ephesians 5:8–11
NKJV

Look carefully then how you walk,
not as unwise men but as wise,
making the most of the time . . .

Ephesians 5:15–16
RSV

. . . be filled with the Spirit,
speaking to one another in psalms and hymns
and spiritual songs,
singing
and making melody in your heart to the Lord,
giving thanks always
for all things
to God the Father
in the name of our Lord Jesus Christ . . .

Ephesians 5:17–20
NKJV

. . . the Lord will reward everyone for whatever
good he does . . .

Ephesians 6:8
NIV

. . . be strong in the Lord, and in the power of
his might.

Ephesians 6:10
KJV

Therefore, put on the full armor of God,
so that when the day of evil comes,
you may be able to stand your ground,

and after you have done everything,
to stand.
Stand firm then,
with the belt of truth buckled around your waist,
with the breastplate of righteousness in place
and with your feet fitted with the readiness
that comes from the gospel of peace.
In addition to all this,
take up the shield of faith,
with which you can extinguish all the flaming
   arrows of the evil one.
Take the helmet of salvation
and the sword of the Spirit,
which is the word of God.
And pray in the Spirit on all occasions
with all kinds of prayers and requests . . .

Ephesians 6:13–18
NIV

PHILIPPIANS

He who has begun a good work in you will perform it . . .

Philippians 1:6
KJVM

And this I pray,
that your love may abound
yet more and more
in knowledge
and in all judgment;
that you may approve things that are excellent;
that you may be sincere and without offense . . .

Philippians 1:9-10
KJVM

Whatever happens, conduct yourselves in a manner worthy of the gospel of Christ . . .

Philippians 1:27
NIV

Do nothing from selfishness or conceit,
but in humility count others better than yourselves.

Let each of you look not only to his own interests,
but also to the interests of others.

Philippians 2:3–4
RSV

. . . work out your own salvation
with fear and trembling.
For it is God who works in you
both to will and to do of his good pleasure.
Do all things without complaining and disputing,
that you may be blameless and harmless,
the sons of God,
without rebuke,
in the midst of a crooked and perverse generation,
among whom you shine as lights in the world,
holding forth the word of life . . .

Philippians 2:13–16
KJVM

. . . one thing I do,
forgetting those things
which are behind
and reaching forward
to those things which are ahead,
I press toward the goal
for the prize
of the upward call
of God in Christ Jesus.

Philippians 3:13–14
NKJV

Rejoice in the Lord always. Again I will say, rejoice!
Let your gentleness be known to all men.
The Lord is at hand.
Be anxious for nothing, but in everything
by prayer and supplication,
with thanksgiving,
let your requests be made known to God;
and the peace of God,
which surpasses all understanding,
will guard your hearts and minds through
    Christ Jesus.

Philippians 4:4–7
NKJV

. . . whatever things are true,
whatever things are honest,
whatever things are just,
whatever things are pure,
whatever things are lovely,
whatever things are of good report;
if there is any excellence,
and if there is anything worthy of praise,
think about these things.

Philippians 4:8
KJVM

I have learned to be content
whatever the circumstances.
I know what it is to be in need,
and I know what it is to have plenty.

I have learned the secret of being content
in any and every situation,
whether well fed or hungry,
whether living in plenty or in want . . .
I can do everything
through him
who gives me strength.

Philippians 4:11–13
NIV

I can do all things through Christ which
strengtheneth me.

Philippians 4:13
KJV

I have received full payment, and more; I am
filled . . .

Philippians 4:18
RSV

. . . my God shall supply all your needs
according to his riches in glory by Christ Jesus.

Philippians 4:19
KJV

COLOSSIANS

All over the world
this gospel is producing fruit and growing,
just as it has been doing among you
since the day you heard it
and understood God's grace
in all its truth.

Colossians 1:6
NIV

. . . we have not ceased to pray for you,
asking that you may be filled
with the knowledge of his will
in all spiritual wisdom and understanding,
to lead a life worthy of the Lord,
fully pleasing to him,
bearing fruit in every good work
and increasing in the knowledge of God.
May you be strengthened with all power,
according to his glorious might,
for all endurance and patience with joy,
giving thanks to the Father,

who has qualified us to share
in the inheritance of the saints
in light.

Colossians 1:9–12
RSV

. . . for in him all things were created,
in heaven and on earth,
visible and invisible,
whether thrones or dominions or principalities
or authorities—
all things were created through him and for him.

Colossians 1:16
RSV

. . . in him
all things
hold together.

Colossians 1:17
RSV

My purpose is that they
may be encouraged in heart
and united in love,
so that they may have the full riches
of complete understanding
in order that they may know the mystery of God,
namely, Christ,
in which are hidden all the treasures
of wisdom and knowledge.

Colossians 2:2–3
NIV

As you have therefore received Christ Jesus the
   Lord,
so walk in Him,
rooted and built up in Him
and established in the faith
as you have been taught,
abounding in it with thanksgiving.

Colossians 2:6–7
NKJV

Set your mind on things above,
not on things on the earth.

Colossians 3:2
NKJV

But now put them all away:
anger, wrath, malice, slander,
and foul talk from your mouth.
Do not lie to one another,
seeing that you have put off
the old nature with its practices
and have put on the new nature,
which is being renewed in knowledge
after the image of its creator.

Colossians 3:8–10
RSV

. . . clothe yourselves with compassion, kindness,
humility, gentleness and patience.
Bear with each other and forgive
whatever grievances you may have

against one another.
Forgive as the Lord forgave you.
And over all these virtues put on love,
which binds them all together
in perfect unity.

Colossians 3:12–14
NIV

And let the peace of God rule in your hearts,
. . . and be thankful.

Let the word of Christ dwell in you richly in
   all wisdom;
teaching and admonishing one another
in psalms and hymns and spiritual songs,
singing with grace in your hearts to the Lord.

And whatever you do in word or deed,
do all in the name of the Lord Jesus,
giving thanks to God and the Father by him.

Colossians 3:15–17
KJVM

Whatever you do,
work at it with all your heart,
as working for the Lord . . .

Colossians 3:23
NIV

THE POSITIVE BIBLE

Continue steadfastly in prayer, being watchful in
it with thanksgiving . . .

Colossians 4:2
RSV

Conduct yourselves wisely toward outsiders,
making the most of the time.
Let your speech always be gracious,
seasoned with salt,
so that you may know
how you ought to answer every one.

Colossians 4:5–6
RSV

He is always wrestling in prayer for you,
that you may stand firm in all the will of God,
mature and fully assured.

Colossians 4:12
NIV

See to it that you complete the work that you
have received in the Lord.

Colossians 4:17
NIV

I THESSALONIANS

We continually remember before our God
and Father
your work produced by faith,
your labor prompted by love,
and your endurance
inspired by hope in our Lord Jesus Christ.

1 Thessalonians 1:3
NIV

. . . we exhorted, and comforted,
and charged every one of you,
as a father does his own children,
that you would walk worthy of God
who calls you into His own kingdom and glory.
For this reason we also thank God without ceasing,
because when you received the word of God
which you heard from us,
you welcomed it not as the word of men,
but as it is in truth, the word of God,
which also effectively works in you who believe.

1 Thessalonians 2:11–13
NKJV

May the Lord make your love increase
and overflow to each other
and for everyone else . . .

1 Thessalonians 3:12
NIV

. . . aspire to live quietly,
to mind your own affairs,
and to work with your hands . . .
so that you may command the respect of
   outsiders,
and be dependent on nobody.

1 Thessalonians 4:11–12
RSV

. . . encourage one another and build one another
up . . .

1 Thessalonians 5:11
RSV

And we urge you, brethren, to recognize those
who labor among you, and are over you in
the Lord and admonish you, and to esteem them
very highly in love for their work's sake. Be at
peace among yourselves.

   Now we exhort you, brethren, warn those who
are unruly, comfort the fainthearted, uphold
the weak, be patient with all.

   See that no one renders evil for evil to any-

one, but always pursue what is good both for
yourselves and for all.

I Thessalonians 5:12–15
NKJV

Rejoice always,
pray without ceasing,
in everything give thanks;
for this is the will of God in Christ Jesus for you.

I Thessalonians 5:16–18
NKJV

Do not quench the Spirit.
Do not despise prophecies.
Test all things; hold fast what is good.
Abstain from every form of evil.
Now may the God of peace Himself
sanctify you completely . . .

I Thessalonians 5:19–23
NKJV

II THESSALONIANS

. . . we constantly pray for you,
that our God may count you worthy of his calling,
and that by his power
he may fulfill
every good purpose of yours
and every act
prompted by your faith.

II Thessalonians 1:11
NIV

May our Lord Jesus Christ himself,
and God, our Father,
who has loved us,
and has given us everlasting consolation
and good hope through grace,
comfort your hearts,
and strengthen you
in every good word and work.

II Thessalonians 2:16–17
KJVM

. . . the Lord is faithful,
he will strengthen you
and keep you safe.

II Thessalonians 3:3
KJVM

Now may the Lord direct your hearts into the love
of God and into the patience of Christ.

II Thessalonians 3:5
NKJV

But as for you, brethren, do not grow weary in
doing good.

II Thessalonians 3:13
NKJV

Now may the Lord of peace Himself give you peace
always in every way.

II Thessalonians 3:16
NKJV

I TIMOTHY

Now the purpose of the commandment is love
from a pure heart,
from a good conscience,
and from sincere faith . . .

I Timothy 1:5
NKJV

Do not rebuke an older man,
but exhort him as a father,
younger men as brothers,
older women as mothers,
younger as sisters,
with all purity.

I Timothy 5:1–2
NKJV

Do not entertain an accusation against an elder
unless it is brought by two or three witnesses.

I Timothy 5:19
NIV

. . . the love of money is the root of all evil . . .

I Timothy 6:10
KJV

. . . flee [evil] and pursue righteousness,
  godliness,
faith, love, patience, gentleness.
Fight the good fight of faith . . .

I Timothy 6:11–12
NKJV

Let them do good, that they be rich in good
  works,
ready to give, willing to share,
storing up for themselves a good foundation for
  the time to come . . .

I Timothy 6:18–19
NKJV

II TIMOTHY

I remind you to fan into flame
the gift of God . . .
For God has not given us the spirit of fear;
but of power,
and of love,
and of a sound mind.

II Timothy 1:7
KJV

. . . be strong
in the grace
that is in Christ Jesus.

II Timothy 2:1
KJV

Study to show thyself approved unto God,
a workman that needeth not be ashamed,
rightly dividing the word of truth.

But shun profane and vain babblings:
for they will increase unto more ungodliness.

II Timothy 2:15–16
KJV

. . . pursue righteousness, faith, love, peace with those who call on the Lord out of a pure heart.

But avoid foolish and ignorant disputes, knowing that they generate strife.

And a servant of the Lord must not quarrel but be gentle to all, able to teach, patient . . .

II Timothy 2:22–24
NKJV

All scripture is God-breathed and is useful for teaching, rebuking, correcting and training in righteousness, so that the man of God may be thoroughly equipped for every good work.

II Timothy 3:16–17
NIV

. . . all deserted me . . .
But the Lord stood by me
and gave me strength . . .
So I was rescued from the lion's mouth.

II Timothy 4:16–17
RSV

TITUS

For the grace of God that brings salvation has appeared to all men, teaching us that, denying ungodliness and worldly lusts, we should live soberly, righteously, and godly in the present age . . .

Titus 2:11–12
NKJV

. . . avoid foolish controversies
. . . and arguments and quarrels . . .
because these are unprofitable and useless.
Warn a divisive person once,
and then warn him a second time,
after that, have nothing to do with him.

Titus 3:9–10
NIV

Our people must learn to devote themselves to doing what is good, in order that they may provide for daily necessities and not live unproductive lives.

Titus 3:14
NIV

PHILEMON

The grace of our Lord Jesus Christ be with
your spirit.

Philemon 1:25
KJV

HEBREWS

The Son is the radiance of God's glory
. . . sustaining all things by his powerful word . . .

Hebrews 1:3
NIV

Nothing in all creation is hidden from God's
sight . . .

Hebrews 4:13
NIV

Let us . . . come boldly unto the throne of grace,
that we may obtain mercy,
and find grace to help in time of need.

Hebrews 4:16
KJV

Land that drinks in the rain often falling on it
and that produces a crop
useful to those for whom it is farmed
receives the blessing of God.

Hebrews 6:7
NIV

God is not unjust;
he will not forget your work
and the love you have shown him
as you have helped his people
and continue to help them.

Hebrews 6:10
NIV

. . . imitate those who through faith and patience
inherit the promises.

Hebrews 6:12
NKJV

This hope we have as an anchor of the soul,
both sure and steadfast . . .

Hebrews 6:19
NKJV

But he [Jesus] holds his priesthood permanently,
because he continues for ever.
    Consequently he is able for all time to save
those who draw near to God through him,
since he always lives to make intercession for
them.

Hebrews 7:24–25
NKJV

Let us hold fast
the confession of our hope
without wavering,
for he who promised is faithful;

and let us consider
how to stir up one another
to love and good works . . .

Hebrews 10:23–24
RSV

Now the just shall live by faith . . .

Hebrews 10:38
KJV

. . . faith is being sure of what we hope for
and certain of what we do not see.

Hebrews 11:1
NIV

But without faith it is impossible to please him:
for he that comes to God
must believe that he exists,
and that he rewards them that diligently seek him.

Hebrews 11:6
KJVM

Therefore, since we are surrounded by
so great a cloud of witnesses,
let us also lay aside every weight,
and sin which clings so closely,
and let us run with perseverance
the race that is set before us.

Hebrews 12:1
RSV

Look to Jesus, the author and finisher of our faith;
who for the joy that was set before him endured the cross, despising the shame, and is set
down at the right hand of the throne of God.

Consider him and how he endured such hostil-
ity from sinners, so that you won't grow weary
and lose resolve.

Hebrews 12:2–3
KJVM

My son, do not make light of the Lord's discipline,
and do not lose heart when he rebukes you,
because the Lord disciplines those he loves . . .

Hebrews 12:5–6
NIV

Endure hardship as discipline; God is treating you
as sons. For what son is not disciplined by
his father? . . .

Hebrews 12:7
NIV

. . . he disciplines us for our good, that we may
share his holiness.

For the moment all discipline seems painful
rather than pleasant; later it yields the peaceful fruit of righteousness to those who have been
trained by it.

Hebrews 12:10–11
RSV

Therefore, strengthen your feeble arms and weak
knees. Make level paths for your feet, so that the
lame may not be disabled, but rather healed.

Hebrews 12:12–13
NIV

Pursue peace with all people, and holiness,
without which no one will see the Lord.

Hebrews 12:14
NKJV

Let brotherly love continue.
Do not forget to entertain strangers
for by so doing
some people have entertained angels
without realizing it.

Hebrews 13:1–2
KJVM

Keep your life free from love of money,
and be content with what you have;
for he has said,
"I will never fail you nor forsake you."

Hebrews 13:5
RSV

So we may boldly say:
"The LORD is my helper;
I will not fear.
What can man do to me?"

Hebrews 13:6
NKJV

Through him then let us continually offer up a
sacrifice of praise to God, that is, the fruit of
lips that acknowledge his name.

Hebrews 13:15
RSV

But do not forget to do good and to share, for
with such sacrifices God is well pleased.

Hebrews 13:16
NKJV

May the God of peace . . .
equip you
with everything good for doing his will,
and may he work
in us
what is pleasing to him.

Hebrews 13:20–21
NIV

JAMES

Count it all joy . . .
when you meet various trials,
for you know that the testing of your faith
produces steadfastness.
And let steadfastness have its full effect,
that you may be perfect and complete,
lacking in nothing.

James 1:2–4
RSV

If any of you lacks wisdom,
let him ask of God,
who gives to all liberally
and without reproach,
and it will be given to him.
But let him ask in faith,
with no doubting,
for he who doubts
is like a wave of the sea
driven and tossed by the wind.

James 1:5–6
NKJV

Every good and perfect gift is from above,
coming down from the Father of heavenly lights,
who does not change like shifting shadows.

James 1:17
NIV

. . . let every person be swift to hear,
slow to speak,
slow to anger:
For in anger a person does not create
the righteousness of God.

James 1:19–20
KJVM

Do not merely listen to the word . . . Do what it
says.

James 1:22
NIV

. . . the man who looks intently
into the perfect law that gives freedom,
and continues to do this,
not forgetting what he has heard,
but doing it—
he will be blessed in what he does.

James 1:25
NIV

Religion that our God and Father accepts as pure
is this: Look after the helpless and don't let
yourself become polluted by the world.

James 1:27
(Compiler's Paraphrase)

. . . a person is justified by what he does, and
not by faith alone.

James 2:24
NIV

Who is wise and understanding among you?
Let him show it by his good life,
by deeds done in the humility
that comes from wisdom . . .

But the wisdom that comes from heaven
is first of all pure;
then peace loving, considerate, submissive,
full of mercy and good fruit,
impartial and sincere.

Peacemakers who sow in peace
raise a harvest of righteousness.

James 3:13, 17–18
NIV

Submit yourselves therefore to God.
Resist the devil, and he will flee from you.
Draw close to God, and he will draw close to
you . . .

James 4:7–8
KJVM

Anyone, then,
who knows they should do good,
and doesn't do it,
sins.

James 4:17
KJVM

Is anyone among you troubled?
Let him pray.
Is anyone cheerful?
Let him sing psalms.

Is anyone among you sick?
Let him call for the elders of the church,
and let them pray over him,
anointing him with oil in the name of the Lord:

And the prayer of faith shall save the sick,
and the Lord will raise him up.
And if he has committed sins,
they will be forgiven.

Confess your faults to one another,
and pray for one another,
that you may be healed.
The fervent prayer of a righteous man
is effective and avails much.

James 5:13–16
KJVM

The effectual fervent prayer of a righteous man availeth much.

James 5:16
KJV

I PETER

Now for a little while you may have had to suffer
grief in all kinds of trials. These have come so
that your faith . . . may be proved genuine and
may result in praise, glory and honor . . .

I Peter 1:6–7
NIV

For it stands in scripture:
"Behold, I am laying in Zion a stone,
a cornerstone chosen and precious,
and he who believes in him
will not be put to shame."

I Peter 2:6
RSV

Live such good lives among the pagans that,
though they accuse you of doing wrong,
they may see your good deeds
and glorify God . . .

I Peter 2:12
NIV

Live as free men,
yet without using your freedom as a pretext
 for evil;
but live as servants of God.

I Peter 2:16
RSV

Finally, all of you,
live in harmony with one another,
be sympathetic,
love as brothers,
be compassionate and humble.

Do not repay evil with evil
or insult with insult;
but with blessing,
because to this you were called
so that you may inherit a blessing.

For, "Whoever would love life
and see good days
must keep his tongue from evil
and his lips from deceitful speech.

He must turn from evil and do good;
he must seek peace and pursue it.

For the eyes of the Lord are on the righteous
and his ears are attentive to their prayer . . ."

I Peter 3:8–12
NIV

And who will harm you
if you become followers of what is good?

But if you should suffer for righteousness' sake,
you are blessed.
Do not be afraid of their terror,
do not be troubled.

But sanctify the Lord God in your hearts,
and always be ready to answer everyone who asks
for a reason for the hope you have.

Respond with gentleness and respect;
having a good conscience,
so that when they speak evil of you,
or your Christian life,
they'll be ashamed.

I Peter 3:13–16
KJVM

Do not live the rest of your earthly life for evil
human desires, but rather for the will of God.

I Peter 4:2
(Compiler's Paraphrase)

Above all hold unfailing your love for one another,
since love covers a multitude of sins.
Practice hospitality ungrudgingly to one another.

As each has received a gift, employ it for one
    another,
as good stewards of God's varied grace . . .
in its various forms.

I Peter 4:8–10
RSV

If anyone speaks, he should do it
as one speaking the very words of God.
If anyone serves, he should do it
with the strength of God,
so that in all things, God may be praised . . .

I Peter 4:11
NIV

God opposes the proud,
but gives grace to the humble.

I Peter 5:5
RSV

Therefore humble yourselves
under the mighty hand of God,
that He may exalt you in due time,
casting all your care upon Him,
for He cares for you.

I Peter 5:6–7
NKJV

And after you have suffered a little while,
the God of all grace,
who has called you to his eternal glory in Christ,

will himself restore, establish, and strengthen you.

I Peter 5:10
RSV

Peace to all who are in Christ Jesus . . .

I Peter 5:14
NKJV

II PETER

Grace and peace be multiplied unto you through
the knowledge of God, and of Jesus our
Lord . . .

II Peter 1:2
KJV

His divine power has given us
everything that we need
for life and godliness
through our knowledge of him
who called us by his own glory and goodness.

Through these he has given us
his very great and precious promises,
so that through them
you may participate in the divine nature
and escape the corruption in the world
caused by evil desires.

For this very reason,
make every effort to add to your faith, goodness;

and to goodness, knowledge;
and to knowledge, self-control,

and to self-control, perseverance;
and to perseverance, godliness

and to godliness, brotherly kindness;
and to brotherly kindness, love . . .

for if you do these things
you will never fall . . .

II Peter 1:3–7, 10
NIV

. . . the Lord knows how to deliver the godly
out of temptations . . .

II Peter 2:9
NKJV

But do not ignore this one fact, beloved,
that with the Lord one day is as a thousand years,
and a thousand years as one day.

The Lord is not slow about his promise
as some count slowness,
but is forbearing toward you,
not wishing that any should perish,
but that all should reach repentance.

II Peter 3:8–9
RSV

You ought to live holy and godly lives
as you look forward to the day of God
and speed its coming.

. . . we are looking forward to a new heaven
and a new earth,
the home of righteousness.
So then, dear friend,
since you are looking forward to this,
make every effort to be found spotless,
blameless
and at peace with him.

II Peter 3:11, 13–14
NIV

I JOHN

This is the message which we have heard from Him and declare to you, that God is light and in Him is no darkness at all.

If we say that we have fellowship with Him, and walk in darkness, we lie and do not practice the truth.

But if we walk in the light as He is in the light, we have fellowship with one another, and the blood of Jesus Christ His Son cleanses us from all sin.

I John 1:5–7
NKJV

He who loves his brother
lives in the light,
and there is nothing in him
to cause him to stumble.

I John 2:10
KJVM

And the world passes away,
along with all the lusts in it;

but one who does the will of God
lives forever.

I John 2:17
KJVM

And you know that He was manifested to take
away our sins, and in Him there is no sin.
Whoever abides in Him does not sin . . .

I John 3:5–6
NKJV

Little children, let no one deceive you.
He who practices righteousness is righteous,
just as He is righteous.
. . . Whoever has been born of God does not sin,
for His seed remains in him;
and he cannot sin,
because he has been born of God.

I John 3:7, 9

For this is the message that you heard from the
beginning, that we should love one another.

I John 3:11
KJVM

Little children, let us not love in word or speech
but in deed and in truth. By this we shall know
that we are of the truth, and reassure our hearts
before him whenever our hearts condemn us; for
God is greater than our hearts, and he knows
everything.

Beloved, if our hearts do not condemn us, we
have confidence before God; and we receive
from him whatever we ask, because we keep his
commandments and do what pleases him.

And this is his commandment, that we should
believe in the name of his Son Jesus Christ
and love one another, just as he has commanded us.

I John 3:18-23
RSV

. . . greater is he that is he that is in you,
than he that is in the world.

I John 4:4
KJV

. . . if we love each other,
God lives in us
and his love is made complete in us.

I John 4:12
NIV

God is love.
Whoever lives in love lives in God,
and God in him.

I John 4:16
NIV

. . . everyone and everything born of God overcomes the world . . .

I John 5:4
KJVM

This is the assurance we have
in approaching God:
that if we ask anything according to his will,
he hears us.
And if we know that he hears us
—whatever we ask—
we know that we have what we asked of him.

I John 5:14–15
NIV

II JOHN

Grace be with you, mercy, and peace,
from God the Father,
and from the Lord Jesus Christ,
the Son of the Father,
in truth and love.

II John 1:3
KJV

As you have heard from the beginning,
his command is that you walk in love.

II John 1:6
NIV

[Hold fast in the faith]
Watch out that you do not lose
what you have worked for,
but that you may be rewarded fully.

II John 1:8
NIV

III JOHN

Beloved, I wish above all things
that you may prosper and be in health,
even as your soul prospers.

III John 1:2
KJVM

Beloved, follow not that which is evil,
but that which is good.
He that does good is of God . . .

III John 1:11
KJVM

JUDE

Mercy, peace, and love be multiplied to you.

Jude 1:2
NKJV

But you, beloved, building yourselves up on your
most holy faith, praying in the Holy Spirit,
keep yourselves in the love of God . . .

Jude 1:20–21
NKJV

Now unto him that is able to keep you from falling,
and to present you faultless
before the presence of his glory
with exceeding joy,
to the only wise God our Savior,
be glory and majesty,
dominion and power,
both now and forever.
Amen.

Jude 1:24–25
KJV

REVELATION

Grace and peace to you from Him who is,
and who was,
and who is to come . . .

Revelation 1:4
NKJV

I know your afflictions and your poverty—yet you
are rich!

Revelation 2:9
NIV

Be faithful,
even to the point of death,
and I will give you the crown of life.

Revelation 2:10
NIV

Wake up!
Strengthen what remains and is about to die,

for I have not found your deeds complete
in the sight of God.

Revelation 3:2
NIV

Then I heard a loud voice saying in heaven, "Now
salvation, and strength, and the kingdom of our
God, and the power of His Christ have come,
for the accuser of our brethren, who accused
them before our God day and night, has been
cast down.

"And they overcame him by the blood of the
Lamb and by the word of their testimony, and
they did not love their lives to the death."

Revelation 12:10–11
NKJV

Alleluia!
Salvation and glory and honor and power
belong to the Lord our God!
For true and righteous are His judgments . . .

And I heard as it were the voice of a great
    multitude,
and as the voice of many waters,
and as the voice of mighty thunderings,
saying, "Alleluia:

for the Lord God omnipotent reigns.
Let us be glad and rejoice, and give honor to
    him . . ."

Revelation 19:6–7
KJVM

. . . and I heard a loud voice from the throne
saying, "Behold, the dwelling of God is with
men. He will dwell with them, and they shall be
his people, and God himself will be with them;
he will wipe away every tear from their eyes, and
death shall be no more, neither shall there be
mourning nor crying nor pain any more, for the
former things have passed away."

Revelation 21:3–4
RSV

There will be no more death or mourning
or crying or pain,
for the old order of things has passed away.

Revelation 21:4
NIV

And he that sat upon the throne said,
Behold; I make all things new.
And he said unto me,
Write for these words are true and faithful.

And he said unto me,
It is done.

I am Alpha and Omega,
the beginning and the end.
I will give unto him that is athirst
of the fountain of the water of life freely.

He that overcomes shall inherit all things;
and I will be his God
and he shall be my son.

Revelation 21: 5-7
KJVM

They will not need the light of a lamp
or the light of the sun,
for the Lord God will give them light . . .

Revelation 22:5
NIV

Behold I am coming soon;
my reward is with me,
and I will give to everyone
according to what he has done.

I am the Alpha and the Omega,
the First and the Last,
the Beginning and the End.

Revelation 22:12-13
NIV

The Spirit [says] . . . "Come!"
And let him who hears say, "Come!"

Whoever is thirsty, let him come;
and whoever wishes,
let him take the free gift of the water of life.

Revelation 22:17
NIV

ALPHABETICAL
SELF-HELP INDEX

*for more than 250 everyday life applications
of* The Positive Bible *scriptures*

All scriptures in *The Positive Bible* are in biblical se-
quence. For a listing of the books of the Bible and the
page numbers on which they can be found, see the table
of contents on page vii.

Use this index and the table of contents to locate helpful verses appropriate to your needs, situations, and challenges at any particular time.

INDEX

Ephesians 3:16–21
Hebrews 13:20–21

• ABUSE

(*See* Courage, Cruelty, Evil, Forgiveness, Goodness, Health, Oppression, Perseverance, Power, Prayer, Protection, Security, Strength, Troubles, Words)

• ACCEPTANCE

Genesis 4:7
I Samuel 12:22
II Kings 18:3
Luke 6:27–28
Luke 6:31
Luke 6:37–38
Colossians 3:12–14

• ACCOMPLISHMENT

(*See* Achievement, Works)

• ACHIEVEMENT

(*See also* Fulfillment)
Exodus 15:2
II Samuel 7:9
I Chronicles 29:12–13
Proverbs 14:23
Isaiah 55:10–13
Matthew 19:26

Mark 9:23
Mark 10:27
John 15:5
John 15:7–9
I Corinthians 9:24
Philippians 4:13

• ACTIONS

(*See* Works)

• ADMIRATION

(*See* Honor)

• AFFLICTION

(*See* Health)

• AFFLUENCE

(*See* Abundance, Finances, Fulfillment)

• AGGRAVATION

(*See* Troubles)

• AILMENT

(*See* Health)

• ALMIGHTY

(*See* Omnipresence)

• ALTRUISM

• ANGER

• ANGUISH

• ANIMOSITY

• ANXIETY/ ANXIOUSNESS

• APPRECIATION

• APPREHENSION

• ARGUING

- ASPIRATION

    (*See* Hope)

- ATTAINMENT

    (*See* Achievement,
    Fulfillment)

- ATTITUDE

    I Samuel 18:14
    I Chronicles 16:8–12
    II Chronicles 27:6
    Psalms 71:14
    Psalms 139:7–10
    Proverbs 3:25–26
    Proverbs 11:25
    Proverbs 11:27
    Proverbs 13:2
    Proverbs 13:7
    Proverbs 14:22
    Proverbs 14:30
    Proverbs 15:4
    Proverbs 15:30
    Proverbs 16:24
    Proverbs 17:22
    Proverbs 19:23
    Proverbs 22:4
    Proverbs 23:7
    Isaiah 52:7
    Amos 5:14–15

Matthew 5:6–9
Matthew 6:20–21
Matthew 6:25–34
Luke 6:20–22
Luke 6:27–28
Luke 6:31
Luke 6:37–38
Acts 13:15
Romans 12:2
Romans 12:12
Romans 12:14–16
II Corinthians 3:3
II Corinthians 10:3–5
Galatians 5:22–23, 25–26
Ephesians 4:22–24
Ephesians 5:1–2
Philippians 1:9–10
Philippians 4:8
Colossians 2:6–7
Colossians 3:2
Colossians 3:12–17
Colossians 3:23
Colossians 4:2
I Thessalonians 5:19–23
I Timothy 6:11–12
I Timothy 6:18–19
II Timothy 1:7
Hebrews 6:12
Hebrews 12:14

II Peter 1:3–7, 10
I John 2:10
III John 1:11

• AUTHORITY

(in the name, in God)
Luke 13:35
John 14:12–14
Acts 4:30

• BEHAVIOR

(*See* Works)

• BEWILDERMENT

(*See* Confusion, Encouragement, Guidance)

• BICKER

(*See* Arguing, Generosity, Love)

• BLESSINGS

Deuteronomy 28:2–13
II Kings 18:5–7
Psalms 145:13–17
Proverbs 22:9
Isaiah 46:4
Jeremiah 29:11–12
Haggai 2:19

Zechariah 8:12–13
Malachi 3:10
Matthew 5:6–9
Luke 6:20–22
Luke 6:37–38
Luke 13:35
John 1:16
Hebrews 13:1–2
I Peter 3:8–12
I Peter 3:13–16

• BOLDNESS

(*See also* Courage, Fear, Strength)
Exodus 15:2
I Chronicles 28:20
Acts 18:9
Hebrews 4:16

• BORN AGAIN

(*See* Renewal)

• BRAVERY

(*See* Boldness, Courage, Faith, Power, Strength)

• BRILLIANCE

(*See* Glory)

- BUSINESS

  Deuteronomy 8:18

  Joshua 1:8–9

  II Samuel 23:3–4

  I Kings 2:2–3

  II Kings 18:3

  I Chronicles 22:13

  I Chronicles 29:12–13

  II Chronicles 13:18

  Proverbs 3:5–6

  Proverbs 3:9–10

  Proverbs 10:4

  Proverbs 11:27

  Proverbs 13:4

  Proverbs 14:23

  Proverbs 16:3

  Proverbs 16:8

  Ecclesiastes 9:10

  Matthew 7:12

  Mark 1:17

  Luke 12:48

  Luke 14:28–30

  Luke 16:10

  Luke 22:26

  Romans 11:36

  Romans 13:7

  Hebrews 13:20–21

- CALM/CALMNESS

  (*See* Peace)

- CAPABILITIES

  (*See* Ability)

- CAREFULNESS

  (*See* Planning, Wisdom)

- CAUTION

  (*See* Money, Planning, Wisdom)

- CELEBRATION

  (*See* Joy, Praise)

- CHARITY

  (*See* Generosity, Giving, Kindness, Love, Thoughtfulness, Works)

- CHASTISEMENT

  (*See* Discipline)

- CHEERFULNESS

  (*See* Attitude, Joy, Praise)

- CHRIST WITHIN

  (*See* Holy Spirit)

- COMFORT

  Exodus 33:14

  I Samuel 12:22

II Samuel 22:2-7
II Samuel 22:17-19
II Samuel 22:26-27
II Samuel 22:29-34
Psalms 9:9
Psalms 30:5
Psalms 34:4-8
Psalms 63:3-8
Psalms 139:7-10
Ecclesiastes 3:1-8
Isaiah 54:10
Isaiah 66:13
Jeremiah 23:23-24
Jeremiah 29:11-12
Daniel 10:12
Matthew 11:28-29
Matthew 18:20
Matthew 28:20
Mark 5:36
John 4:14
John 10:10
II Corinthians 1:3-4
Ephesians 2:14
Philippians 4:11-13
I Thessalonians 2:11-13
II Thessalonians 2:16-17
II Timothy 1:7
I Peter 5:6-7
I Peter 5:10

Jude 1:2
Revelation 21:3-4
Revelation 22:12-13
Revelation 22:17

• COMFORTER
(*See* Holy Spirit)

• COMMAND(ING)
(*See* Authority, Power)

• COMMENTS
(*See* Words)

• COMMUNICATE
(*See* Attitude, Prayer, Words, Works)

• COMPASSION
(*See* Comfort, Generosity, Giving, Help, Kindness, Love, Thoughtfulness, Works)

• COMPETENCE
(*See* Ability)

• CONDEMNATION
Luke 6:27-28
Luke 6:31

Luke 6:37–38
Romans 8:1
Romans 12:14
I John 3:18–23
Revelation 12:10–11

- CONFIDENCE
  Exodus 16:18
  II Samuel 7:9
  Psalms 118:5–17
  Proverbs 3:25–26
  Isaiah 43:1–2
  Matthew 6:25–34
  Matthew 19:26
  Matthew 28:20
  Mark 9:23
  Mark 10:27
  Luke 1:37
  Philippians 4:13
  Hebrews 13:6
  I John 3:18–23

- CONFINEMENT
  (*See* Oppression)

- CONFUSION
  Proverbs 3:5–6
  Proverbs 3:21–24
  Isaiah 50:7

Romans 16:17
II Timothy 1:7

- CONQUERING
  (*See* Overcoming)

- CONSCIENTIOUSNESS
  (*See* Attitude, Perseverance,
  Righteousness, Spirituality,
  Works)

- CONSIDERATE
  (*See* Generosity, Help,
  Kindness, Love, Thought-
  fulness, Works)

- CONSOLATION
  (*See* Comfort, Encouragement, Grief)

- CONTENTMENT
  (*See also* Patience)
  Philippians 4:11–13

- CONTROL
  (*See* Power)

- CORRUPTION
  (*See* Fairness, Honesty)

INDEX

Matthew 28:20
Luke 6:20–22
John 15:19
John 16:33
Romans 13:12
II Corinthians 4:17–18
II Corinthians 5:7
II Corinthians 5:17
II Corinthians 6:4–10
Philippians 4:8
I Thessalonians 5:19–23
II Thessalonians 2:16–17
II Thessalonians 3:3
Revelation 21:3-4

• DESPONDENCY

(*See* Attitude, Depression,
Discouragement, Doubt,
Encouragement, Faith,
Grief, Health)

• DETERMINATION

(*See* Perseverance)

• DEVOTION

(*See* Faith, Praise, Prayer)

• DIFFICULTIES

(*See* Overcoming, Troubles)

• DIGNITY

(*See* Honor)

• DIRECTION

(*See* Guidance)

• DISAPPOINTMENT

(*See* Attitude, Depression,
Discouragement, Doubt,
Encouragement, Faith,
Grief, Health)

• DISASTER

(*See* Comfort, Discipline,
Encouragement, Faith, Ful-
fillment, Goodness, Grief,
Material Needs, Oppression,
Patience, Perseverance,
Protection, Renewal, Secu-
rity, Troubles, Worry)

• DISCERNING

(*See* Wisdom)

• DISCIPLINE/
SELF-CONTROL

Proverbs 13:18
Ecclesiastes 11:6
Isaiah 7:9
John 15:1–2
II Corinthians 12:7–8
Galatians 5:13

Ephesians 4:29
Philippians 1:9–10
Colossians 2:2–3
Colossians 3:15–17
I Thessalonians 2:11–13
I Thessalonians 5:11–15
Hebrews 10:23–24
Revelation 2:9

• ENDURANCE
(*See* Patience,
Perseverance)

• ENTHUSIASM
(*See* Encouragement, Joy)

• ENVY
(*See* Jealousy, Kindness,
Love)

• ERROR
(*See* Evil)

• ESTEEM
(*See* Honor)

• ETHICS
(*See* Fairness, Honesty,
Jealousy)

• EVERLASTING
(*See* Omnipresence)

• EVIL
(overcoming)
Genesis 4:7
Exodus 33:13
Joshua 1:5
II Samuel 22:2–7
II Samuel 22:17–19
Job 8:20–21
Psalms 37:7–9
Psalms 140:1–2
Proverbs 4:14–18
Proverbs 4:24–27
Proverbs 11:27
Proverbs 14:19
Jeremiah 15:20–21
Amos 5:14–15
Matthew 5:44–46
Matthew 10:16
Matthew 12:34–35
Matthew 18:18
Luke 6:37–38
Romans 8:31
Romans 8:35, 37
Romans 12:17
Romans 12:21
Romans 16:17
Romans 16:19

I Corinthians 15:33
II Corinthians 6:4–10
II Corinthians 10:3–5
Ephesians 6:13–18
Philippians 1:27
I Thessalonians 5:19–23
James 4:7–8
I Peter 3:8–12
I John 3:5–6
I John 3:7, 9

Proverbs 16:8
Proverbs 31:8–9
Hosea 12:6
Obadiah 1:15
Micah 6:8
Matthew 7:12
Luke 6:27–28
Luke 6:31
Luke 6:37–38
Romans 13:7

• EXALT

(*See* Joy, Praise, Prayer, Thankfulness)

• EXPECTATIONS

(*See* Hope)

• FAIRNESS

(*See also* Love, Generosity)
Deuteronomy 16:19
II Samuel 22:26–27
I Kings 3:9
II Kings 18:3
Psalms 15:1–5
Psalms 37:7–9
Psalms 62:11–12
Psalms 112:5–6
Proverbs 2:3–12
Proverbs 4:14–18

• FAITH

Genesis 18:14
Genesis 22:14
I Samuel 12:22
I Samuel 12:24
II Chronicles 20:20
Job 11:13–19
Psalms 1:1–3
Psalms 91:9–16
Psalms 112:7–9
Proverbs 2:3–12
Proverbs 3:3–4
Proverbs 23:19
Proverbs 24:10
Ecclesiastes 11:1
Isaiah 7:9
Daniel 10:12
Matthew 6:25–34

• FEAR

INDEX

INDEX

INDEX

Philemon 1:25
Hebrews 4:16
II Peter 1:2
II John 1:3

- ## GRATEFULNESS
  (*See* Praise, Thankfulness)

- ## GRATITUDE
  (*See* Praise, Thankfulness)

- ## GRIEF
  (*See also* Comfort, Peace)
  Nehemiah 8:10
  Job 5:7–11
  Psalms 30:5
  Ecclesiastes 3:1–8
  Isaiah 61:1–3
  Jeremiah 31:3–4
  Jeremiah 31:12–13
  Matthew 5:4
  II Thessalonians 3:16
  I Peter 1:6–7
  I Peter 5:6–7
  I Peter 5:10
  Revelation 21:3–4

- ## GUIDANCE
  (*See also* Holy Spirit, Mystical Knowledge)

Genesis 26:24
Exodus 33:13
Leviticus 9:4
Deuteronomy 31:8
Joshua 1:5
Joshua 1:8–9
II Chronicles 15:2
II Chronicles 16:9
II Chronicles 27:6
Ezra 8:22
Job 5:17–18
Job 32:8–9
Psalms 43:3
Psalms 121:1–3
Psalms 139:7–10
Psalms 145:18–20
Proverbs 2:3–12
Proverbs 3:5–6
Proverbs 3:21–24
Isaiah 30:20–21
Isaiah 42:16
Isaiah 58:9–11
Isaiah 64:8
Jeremiah 18:3–6
Daniel 9:22–23
Matthew 7:12
John 14:16–17
John 14:26
John 16:12–13
Acts 2:25–26

INDEX

Acts 14:17
Romans 14:17–19
Philippians 4:4–7
I Thessalonians 5:16–18
James 1:2–4
Revelation 19:6–7

• JUSTICE

(*See* Fairness, Honesty)

• KINDNESS

Proverbs 10:19
Proverbs 11.17
Proverbs 12:25
Proverbs 14:21
Proverbs 14:31
Proverbs 15:1
Proverbs 19:17
Matthew 7:12
Acts 14:17
Romans 14:17–19
Romans 15:1–2
Galatians 5:22–23, 25–26
Ephesians 4:31–32
I Thessalonians 5:12–15
I Timothy 6:18–19
II Timothy 2:22–24
I Peter 3:8–12
II Peter 1:3–7, 10

• KNOWLEDGE/ LEARNING

Proverbs 16:20
Proverbs 17:27
Proverbs 19:2
Proverbs 19:8
Proverbs 19:20
Proverbs 22:17–18
Proverbs 23:12
Ecclesiastes 8:7
II Timothy 2:15–16

• LABOR

(*See* Works)

• LEARNING

(*See* Knowledge)

• LIGHT

(*See also* Holy Spirit, Mystical Knowledge)
Genesis 1:3–4
Psalms 27:1
Psalms 36:7–10
Psalms 43:3
Psalms 89:15–17
Psalms 112:4
Psalms 119:105
Psalms 139:11–12

INDEX

Colossians 3:12–14
I Thessalonians 2:11–13
I Thessalonians 3:12
I Thessalonians 5:12–15
II Thessalonians 2:16–17
II Thessalonians 3:5
I Timothy 1:5
I Timothy 6:11–12
II Timothy 1:7
II Timothy 2:22–24
Hebrews 10:23–24
I Peter 3:8–12
II Peter 1:2–10
I John 2:10
I John 3:11
I John 3:18–23
I John 4:12
I John 4:16
II John 1:3
II John 1:6
Jude 1:20–21

- ## LURE
  (*See* Temptation)

- ## MAGNIFY
  (*See* Praise)

- ## MAJESTY
  (*See* Glory)

- ## MASTERY
  (*See* Fulfillment, Perseverance, Power)

- ## MATERIAL NEEDS
  (*See also* Abundance, Finances, Fulfillment)
  Deuteronomy 28:2–13
  Psalms 16:5
  Psalms 34:9–10
  Psalms 65:9–13
  Psalms 128:1–2
  Proverbs 3:9–10
  Joel 2:21–24
  Joel 2:26
  Haggai 2:19
  Zechariah 8:12
  Matthew 7:7–8
  Luke 6:37–38
  Luke 12:29–31
  II Corinthians 9:6–8, 10–11
  Ephesians 5:15–16
  Philippians 4:19
  Hebrews 13:20–21
  II Peter 1:3–7, 10

- ## MISTREATMENT
  (*See* Evil, Kindness, Oppression, Patience, Protection)

Jeremiah 32:27

Luke 1:37

Acts 17:24–35

Acts 17:28

Romans 11:36

Hebrews 1:3

Hebrews 4:13

Hebrews 7:24–25

I John 2:17

I John 3:18–23

Revelation 1:4

Revelation 21:5–7

Revelation 22:12–13

• ONENESS

John 17:20–21

Acts 4:31–32

Romans 8:38–39

Romans 10:12

Romans 11:36

I Corinthians 12:4–12

I Corinthians 12:20, 26

Ephesians 4:11–13

Colossians 1:17

I John 4:12

I John 4:16

Revelation 21:3–4

Revelation 21:5–7

• OPPRESSION

(*See also* Comfort, Courage, Discipline, Encouragement, Evil, Faith, Patience, Perseverance, Strength)

Exodus 1:12

Exodus 33:14

II Samuel 22:2–7

II Samuel 22:17–19

Job 36:8–11

Psalms 9:9

Psalms 34:4–8

Psalms 37:1–4

Psalms 91:9–16

Proverbs 14:31

Proverbs 31:8–9

Isaiah 52:2

Joel 3:16

Nahum 1:13

Matthew 5:44–46

John 8:32

Romans 8:31

Romans 8:35, 37

II Corinthians 6:4–10

II Corinthians 10:3–5

• OPTIMISM

(*See* Attitude, Encouragement, Hope, Faith, Spirituality)

• OVERCOMING

Genesis 4:7

• PEACE

• PERFORMANCE
(*See* Works)

• PERPLEXED
(*See* Confusion, Encouragement, Guidance)

• PERSECUTION
(*See* Oppression, Troubles)

• PERSEVERANCE

Psalms 51:10

Proverbs 4:24–27

Proverbs 10:4

Proverbs 12:24

Proverbs 13:4

Proverbs 13:12

Proverbs 21:5

Proverbs 24:10

Proverbs 24:30–34

Ecclesiastes 7:8

Ecclesiastes 11:6

Isaiah 7:9

Haggai 2:4–5

Mark 14:38

Luke 12:35–36

Acts 2:25–26

Romans 5:1–5

Romans 12:9–11

Romans 12:12

I Corinthians 15:58

II Corinthians 6:4–10

Galatians 6:9–10

Ephesians 6:13–18

Philippians 3:13–14

Colossians 1:9–12

Colossians 4:17

II Thessalonians 3:5

II Thessalonians 3:13

I Timothy 6:11–12

Hebrews 10:23–24

Hebrews 12:1

James 1:2–4

James 1:25

I Peter 5:10

II Peter 1:3–7, 10

II John 1:8

Revelation 2:10

• PERSISTENCE

(*See* Perseverance)

• PESSIMISM

(*See* Attitude, Depression, Discouragement, Doubt, Encouragement, Faith, Grief)

• PLANNING

Proverbs 13:12

Proverbs 13:16

Proverbs 14:8

Proverbs 14:15

Proverbs 14:22

Proverbs 19:2

Proverbs 20:4

Proverbs 20:18

Proverbs 21:5

Jeremiah 29:11–12
Luke 14:28–30
Philippians 4:4–7

- POLITENESS

  (*See* Kindness, Thoughtfulness, Words)

- POWER

  (*See also* Authority)
  II Samuel 5:10
  Daniel 2:20–22
  Micah 3:8
  Matthew 17:20
  Matthew 18:18–19
  Luke 22:26
  John 13:3
  Ephesians 1:17–20
  Ephesians 3:16–21
  Ephesians 6:10
  Colossians 1:9–12
  II Timothy 1:7

- PRAISE

  Exodus 15:2
  I Chronicles 16:8–12
  I Chronicles 16:23–25
  I Chronicles 29:11
  Psalms 63:3–8
  Psalms 71:14

Psalms 89:15–17
Isaiah 64:4–5
Daniel 2:20–22
Daniel 4:3
Daniel 6:26–27
Joel 2:13
Joel 2:26
Amos 4:13
Ephesians 5:17–20
Colossians 2:6–7
Hebrews 1:3
Hebrews 13:15
James 5:13–16
I Peter 1:6–7
Jude 1:24–25
Revelation 19:6–7

- PRAYER

  II Kings 20:5
  I Chronicles 16:8–12
  I Chronicles 16:27
  II Chronicles 33:12–13
  Job 5:7–11
  Jeremiah 33:3
  Daniel 9:19
  Daniel 9:22–23
  Matthew 7:7–8
  Mark 11:22–24
  Mark 14:38

Ephesians 6:13–18
II Thessalonians 3:3
II Peter 1:3–7, 10

• PRUDENCE

(*See* Wisdom)

• RAGE

(*See* Anger)

• REASSURANCE

(*See* Encouragement)

• REBIRTH

(*See* Renewal)

• REFUGE

(*See* Courage, Peace, Protection, Security)

• REGENERATE

(*See* Renewal)

• REJOICE

(*See* Joy, Praise)

• REJUVENATE

(*See* Renewal)

• RELAX

(*See* Peace)

• REMAKE

(*See* Renewal)

• RENEWAL/ SALVATION

Isaiah 43:18–19
Isaiah 44:22
Isaiah 51:11
Isaiah 52:2
Jeremiah 15:19
Jeremiah 18:3–6
Ezekiel 36:26
Daniel 4:25–27
Hosea 14:4
Joel 2:28–32
Nahum 1:13
Zephaniah 2:7
Zephaniah 3:17
Haggai 2:19
Zechariah 8:13
Matthew 7:7–8
Mark 8:34–37
Romans 6:4
Romans 6:6
Romans 12:2
Galatians 1:3

- SADNESS

  (*See* Attitude, Depression, Discouragement, Doubt, Encouragement, Faith, Grief, Health, Joy)

- SAFEKEEPING

  (*See* Protection, Security)

- SAGACITY

  (*See* Wisdom)

- SAGE

  (*See* Wisdom)

- SALVATION

  (*See* Renewal)

- SAVVY

  (*See* Wisdom)

- SCARED

  (*See* Courage, Fear)

- SCHOLARSHIP

  (*See* Knowledge)

- SECURITY

  (*See also* Courage, Peace, Protection)

Exodus 33:14
Leviticus 26:4
Leviticus 26:6
I Samuel 12:22
Psalms 145:13–17
Jeremiah 33:6

- SELF-ASSURANCE

  (*See* Confidence, Boldness, Encouragement, Faith)

- SELF-CONTROL

  (*See* Discipline, Patience, Perseverance, Strength, Temptation)

- SELF-RELIANCE

  (*See* Boldness, Courage, Strength)

- SELFISHNESS

  (*See* Generosity, Giving, Help, Kindness, Love, Thoughtfulness, Works)

- SERVE, SERVICE

  (*See* Generosity, Help, Works)

- SHIELD

  (*See* Protection, Security)

- SICKNESS

    (*See* Health)

- SIN

    (*See* Goodness, Overcoming, Righteousness, Temptation)

- SORROW

    (*See also* Comfort, Grief, Trouble)
    Job 5:17–18
    Psalms 34:18
    Nahum 1:7
    Zephaniah 2:7

- SPEAKING

    (*See* Words)

- SPIRITUALITY

    Job 5:17–18
    Psalms 34:18
    Nahum 1:7
    Zephaniah 2:7
    Acts 17:28
    Romans 2:6–7, 10
    Romans 6:13
    Romans 8:5–6
    Romans 8:10
    Romans 8:14–15

Romans 12:2
I Corinthians 14:15
II Corinthians 3:3
II Corinthians 6:4–10
II Corinthians 6:16
Ephesians 5:15–20
Ephesians 6:13–18
Colossians 1:9–12
I Thessalonians 5:16–18
I Thessalonians 5:19–23
Hebrews 13:20–21
I Peter 2–10

- SPLENDOR

    (*See* Glory)

- SPOKEN

    (*See* Words)

- STABILITY

    Psalms 51:10
    Psalms 139:7–10
    Proverbs 13:11
    Colossians 1:17
    James 1:17

- STEWARDSHIP

    (*See* Business, Honesty, Money, Planning, Trust, Wisdom)

- THANKFULNESS

  (*See also* Praise)
  Colossians 1:9–12
  Colossians 2:6–7
  Colossians 3:15–17
  Colossians 4:2
  I Thessalonians 5:16–18

- THOUGHTFULNESS

  Proverbs 10:19
  Proverbs 11:17
  Proverbs 11:25
  Jeremiah 22:16
  Matthew 7:12
  Romans 12:17–18
  Romans 13:7
  Romans 14:8, 13
  Romans 15:1–2
  Colossians 3:12–14
  I Timothy 5:1–2

- THREATS

  (*See* Evil, Overcoming,
  Troubles)

- TITHE. TITHING

  (*See* Abundance, Finances,
  Fulfillment, Generosity,
  Giving)

- TOIL

  (*See* Works)

- TOLERANCE

  (*See* Acceptance)

- TRANQUILLITY

  (*See* Peace)

- TRIUMPH

  (*See* Success)

- TROUBLES

  (*See also* Anxiety, Worry)
  Exodus 15:2
  I Samuel 26:24
  II Samuel 16:12
  II Samuel 22:2–7
  Job 5:17–18
  Job 36:8–11
  Psalms 9:9
  Psalms 17:8–9
  Psalms 23:1–6
  Psalms 34:4–8
  Psalms 34:17–18
  Psalms 71:14–23
  Proverbs 24:1–2
  Proverbs 24:10
  Isaiah 26:12
  Isaiah 30:20–21

INDEX

INDEX

• WORRY

Luke 12:6–7
Luke 12:22–31
Luke 21:14–15
John 14:1
John 14:27
Philippians 4:4–7
I Peter 5:6–7

● WORSHIP

(*See* Praise, Prayer,
Thankfulness)

● WRATH

(*See* Anger)